Underwriting Dreams

A Journery of Leadership and Hope

OUSMANE KABRÉ

Copyright © 2024 Ousmane Kabre LLC

All rights reserved

No part of this book may be reproduced, or stored in a retrieval system, or transmitted in any form or by any means, electronic, mechanical, photocopying, recording, or otherwise, without express written permission of the publisher.

ISBN-13: 979-8-9904064-3-8

*Cover design by: Ben Elikem and Kim Gillett
Printed in the United States of America*

Underwriting Dreams

This book is lovingly dedicated to my Mother, Mariam Kaboré, who was my first teacher, my ultimate inspiration, and my guiding light from the very beginning, and to my father, Sayouba Kabré, who instilled in me the values of perseverance, the importance of integrity, and the significance of giving back to the community. Their unwavering support and belief in me have shaped the person I am today.

"It's about investing in the potential of human ambition. It's the belief in turning the intangible into the tangible, the extraordinary into the achievable, and the dreams of today into the realities of tomorrow."

– *Muchia*

Contents

Prologue iv

*1. From Homemade Cakes to Classroom Sales:
An Entrepreneur in the Making* 3

2. Crossing Continents for a Dream 25

*3. Paying It Forward for Global Change:
The Power of Vision and Goals* 41

4. Breakfast Meetings 59

*5. Partnerships, Collaborations, and
Strategic Decisions* 69

*6. Leadership, Education, and
Entrepreneurship* 87

*7. Beyond Dreams:
The Power of Goal Setting* 115

8. Fueling Change with Resilience 129

9. Transforming Tomorrow 143

*10 Horizons of Hope: Building Africa's
Next Generation of Chenge Agents* 153

Acknowledgments 159

Prologue

It was the summer of 1997 in Burkina Faso, Africa, and we had just gotten out of school on summer vacation. I was six years old, the middle child of seven siblings. I asked my Mom if I could visit my Grandmother in Karpala for the summer. Reluctant to grant permission, she worried that it was a large, sparsely populated area with no electricity (except for the homes of a few wealthy individuals who could afford a generator). She feared that I would be walking around an unfamiliar community in the dark. My grandmother lived with my mother's younger brother, Ousmane, and so my Mom knew I would be well cared for, so she decided to let me go.

Like most six-year-olds coming from a more developed area, I didn't quite understand what it would be like to live without electricity (no lights, no running water, nothing) until I fully experienced it. But I can tell you it didn't take long to know how truly inconvenient it was to live like that. However, Being the determined boy I was, I quickly figured out how to use this to my advantage.

As you'll learn in this book, from a young age, when my mind was set on something, there was no turning back. I knew what I wanted, and I was determined to get it — "no" was not an option.

You'll also learn that I've always had a drive to make money — except the meaning and reason behind making money means something much different today than it did back then (thankfully!)

So, at age six, I took our inconvenient living situation of no electricity and turned it into a business opportunity (Yes, you read that right, at age 6!). I realized I could walk to the city, buy a couple of liters of lamp kerosene, and sell it for more than what I paid. I could sell oil to everyone in my grandmother's neighborhood, and they would no longer have to live in the dark.

It was a fantastic idea, and I was so excited that I stayed up all night, planning every single detail of my new business — from where I would buy the kerosene, how I would sell it, and who I would sell it to. I couldn't wait to tell my grandmother what a genius I was. Finally, around 7:30 am, everyone woke up. Grandmother had prepared porridge for breakfast. Afterward, I asked her if I could share my business idea. I had everything perfectly laid out (just as any six-year-old can have a business plan laid out!). We sat at the kitchen table, and I carefully explained every detail to her. I wanted her to see that I knew what I was doing and was sure it would work.

Grandma sat there patiently, listening to each word, nodding her head, and saying nothing. With her stoic face, I couldn't tell if she was on to my idea or if it wasn't any good at all. The suspense was killing me (especially for a boy at the age of 6 who didn't have much patience at all!)

Finally, Grandma smiled, proud of the elaborate plan I had devised. Like any good mentor (and grandmother), she asked me a few questions but was hesitant to say "yes" at first.She thought I was much too young to handle money, let alone walk the streets unattended in a new unfamiliar area.

However, as I mentioned earlier, "no" wasn't the answer I was looking for. So, I managed to convince her with the persuasion skills I had learned at my young age.

She agreed to lend me money to start my business

— but it was under one condition: one of my uncles, Abdoulaye, who was about my age and living in the house, was to follow me on my first day of business. She was worried about me getting lost in the neighborhood. I had done that once before!

The following day, I woke up at 6:00 am, ready for the first day of my new business. Grandma loaned me fifty cents to start. When Abdoulaye was ready, we headed to the city, Ouagadougou. It was a two-hour walk to the town that took us through a variety of landscapes, from stretches of sparse vegetation where the sun cast its unyielding gaze to miles of farmland where families were working tirelessly. The air was warm and carried the scent of dry earth and the occasional smell of wildflowers that dotted the landscape.

As we approached the town, the sounds of life grew louder: children's laughter echoing from behind compound walls and the distant murmur of conversation. The roads, once mere dirt paths, now bore the marks of more frequent passage—compacted earth and scattered stones that told of many journeys like ours.

Entering the outskirts of Ouagadougou, the streets became busier, lined with makeshift stalls where vendors sold everything from fruits and vegetables to colorful textiles. The architecture evolved too, from simple, mud-brick homes to more solid, varied structures. The air buzzed with the sounds of motorcycles weaving through traffic, the calls of street vendors, and the blend of music floating from open windows.

We went to the local gas station, Total Energies. We bought two liters of oil. Then we began our two-hour return home to start selling the Kerosene.

At 5:00 pm, around dusk, we went door to door, asking people if they needed our service. Some people appreciated the ask and wanted us to return the next day; some said "no", but we sold our first two liters of kerosene. We returned home that night with an empty container, excited to go back out the next day.

Grandma recommended that I find a small milk box and save at least 10% of my profit to buy school supplies and new clothes. I went from selling two liters the first day to five liters each day for the remainder of the summer. The people in the neighborhood were thankful for my service, and I was grateful for their support. By the end of summer, I had enough money saved in my milk jug to buy new clothes, a pair of jeans, and shoes for school! I couldn't wait to tell my mother about the booming business I started. She would be so proud of me. I knew Mother would be thankful that she didn't have to pay for my new clothes this school year. It would save her money, and I could get what I wanted — I just needed her help at the market, for she knew how to bargain, and I hadn't quite learned that skill.

This was the first time I had felt the exhilaration of being resilient and determined. It was my first experience in my entrepreneurial journey, and I learned about the power of ideas.

My personal experience underscores the deep impact of initiative and self-reliance. It demonstrates that with creativity, hard work, and a willingness to serve others, we can transform humble beginnings into rewarding achievements. This journey illustrates the significance of entrepreneurship: the ability to see opportunities where others see obstacles to create value from challenges.

We should remember that every successful venture starts with a single step, a bold idea, and the courage to act upon it. It is my sincere hope that this story stand as a testament to the power of believing in ourselves and pursuing our goals with determination. I encourage you to embrace this lesson as you face future challenges: where there is perseverance, there is reward; where there is vision, there is

"I saw it ...a gateway to understanding the world in its plurality and complexity..."

1

From Homemade Cakes to Classroom Sales: An Entrepreneur in the Making

As the sun dipped below the horizon, casting hues of orange and pink over the vast Savannah of Burkina Faso, my family and I settled into our modest yet warm and inviting home. It was a blend of traditional structures and modern cement constructions. Its walls were a fusion of mud-brick and cement, coated with a natural plaster that glowed softly under the fading light. The house was thoughtfully designed with a central hub where we would gather for meals, share stories, and admire the stars at night.

This open-air space brought the family together, nurturing a sense of community and openness within our home. Inside, the rooms were simple, with floors covered with handwoven mats and walls decorated with colorful textiles. These elements brought life and warmth to the earthy tones of the mud-brick and cement walls. The thick walls kept it pleasantly cool and provided respite from the heat.

The kitchen area, slightly apart from the main living spaces, had a mix of traditional clay stoves and modern appliances. There, you would often find my mother preparing meals rich in local flavors. Bordering this, my mother grew a small garden offering fresh vegetables and herbs and connecting us to the land and seasons.

As I think back to the memories of my childhood home, I'm filled with love, laughter, and the shared joys and challenges of life.

Summer was ending, and we were preparing to return to school for the semester.

I was now seven years old, and at that time, Burkina Faso was a predominantly agricultural economy marked by subsistence farming and economic struggles. Children and families faced the harsh realities of poverty and income inequality.

The era was characterized by a political landscape in transition following the assassination of President

Thomas Sankara in 1987, leading to a period of civil unrest with demands for political reforms. The educational system wrestled with issues of access and quality.

Many children encountered barriers to education, particularly in rural areas where factors such as limited infrastructure, distance to schools, and socioeconomic constraints hindered learning opportunities. Girls faced additional hurdles due to gender disparities, cultural norms, and early marriage.

Despite these challenges, Burkina Faso implemented various educational policies, reflecting a commitment to addressing the complex economic and social factors influencing the upbringing of its children during this transformative period.

As a seven-year-old boy, I never once felt like we were poor or disadvantaged. It was just the way of life, and we knew nothing else. We didn't have technology, computers, or the internet to see what we didn't have — or how life was different in other parts of the world.

My parents did well for themselves and our family. My father wore multiple hats: he was a religious leader, a farmer, a small business owner, and a real estate investor (he owned a few properties and received monthly income from the tenants.) My mother owned a successful business selling homemade cakes. I credit much of my drive and determination to them, especially my mother. My parents' multifaceted roles in the community were not just a means of livelihood but a powerful lesson about leadership, resilience, and entrepreneurship.

Their ability to balance multiple responsibilities while contributing significantly to our family's well-being and the community's prosperity was nothing short of inspiring. They always demonstrated the daily power of hard work, integrity, and perseverance. It wasn't just about making money but about creating value and making a difference in the lives of others. Watching my parents navigate the challenges and triumphs of running a business imbued me with a deep sense of purpose and an understanding of the impact one can make through dedication and passion. Most of all, they taught me the importance of staying true to one's vision despite the obstacles.

My mother had a successful business selling homemade cakes. Her company was profitable, and she frequently hired young people who came to the city from nearby villages looking for work. Some even came with a recommendation and a person of reference from relatives on my father's side. Others were just young folks looking for something to do to earn extra money.

Her employee turnover rate was low. She offered them fair compensation, treated them well, gave them a place to live at no charge, and took care of the evening meals. For breakfast, her employees would have free cakes with hot porridge. My mother always added an extra cake on top of the regular count. An intelligent employee would sell the extra cakes, spend a small portion for lunch, and save the rest. A not-so-smart employee would save the cakes for themselves.

In addition, all her employees had monthly base pay that increased depending on sales performance and length of employment. Two of her employees had been on the payroll for over five years and had become family to us.

Most employees typically left around age 22, but the older they were, the more uncomfortable it was to carry a big wooden box with cakes on their heads and walk through the town.

Later that year, I had been looking forward to spending another Summer at my grandmother's house to build on the business I had started the year before. However, my mother didn't give me permission to go this time. She had a different plan for me. Recognizing my great potential as a salesman from my time selling kerosene at my grandmother's, she wanted to test my abilities for her business, so she hired me to sell her homemade cakes.

Instead of being on her payroll, I insisted that I work only on a commission basis. My mom agreed to the terms. She knew that I would be treated the same way as everyone else, for she was not only my employer but also my accountant and banker.

The plan was to hit the downtown marketplace around 6:30 a.m. when the cake was still hot and travelers were looking for something to eat before leaving for their trip. My first day wasn't very successful; I returned home with some cakes. Usually, cakes from the day before could not be resold the next day. My mom asked me to return to the marketplace in the evening and sell them at a discount of two for the price of one to new travelers who had just arrived. They were tired and might be looking for something cheap to eat. I followed her advice and returned with no cakes. It did not take me too long to sell the leftovers, for people loved the bargain.

The first week was challenging, but over time, I got used to my new business venture — in fact, I got really good at it. I identified the best places and times to reach a specific group of customers. For instance, I learned that around 11:00 a.m., I needed to be at the supermarket, "Roodwooko." In this public market, quick research revealed that my customers were frugal entrepreneurs. I also noticed that around 3:00 p.m., when the cakes were no longer fresh, older people loved to buy and eat them with "Zoom-Koom," a local drink.

I did exceptionally well that summer and was very proud of myself. I became so passionate about selling products and making a profit that I decided I should make a profit all year long. Why should I wait until the end of summer to start working again? So, I negotiated a deal with my mother.

I told my mother that she could spend the first two hours of her morning routines just focusing on two of her three main activities (getting her employees ready to hit the marketplace with hotcakes and selling porridge to our neighbors), and I would take care of her third activity; selling oranges, special home cakes, and sandwiches for kids at my primary school.

My mom thought it was a good idea. She estimated that she could get more business since almost everyone in my school knew me and also knew that my mom was selling food in the morning and during the breaks. She was correct; my popularity in school indeed attracted more clientele. I was remarkably active in school, often elected as class president, drafted to join the local soccer team very early, and became the team captain. Almost everyone knew me in the neighborhood.

I helped my mother prepare in the morning before class. As soon as she had sent off her employees to the marketplace, she began serving our neighbors her homemade porridge, and I ran off to class. My second shift started at 9:45 a.m. when one of the schoolboys rang the bell for the 30-minute break. I always looked forward to the bell ringing. It was go time! I left class as soon as possible and returned to my station to serve my classmates.

Many of the school teachers had also noticed my new routine, got to know my mom, and would often place orders with me. My older brothers would make fun of me because they thought this was a female job. It did not bother me. I paid less attention to their comments and enjoyed the service that I was providing, not just to the customers but to my mother. I knew that my mom was working hard for her family and deserved some help from her children. Plus, I also got to make money to buy whatever I needed or wanted.

Of course, like all children at the age of 7, there were times when my friends would be playing soccer, and I had to help my mother instead of playing with them. In those times, it felt like a burden. Looking back, those experiences instilled in me the work ethic, dreams of entrepreneurship, resiliency, and so much more. It wasn't a burden or a hindrance but an opportunity (*I was just too young to realize it.*)

The time that I spent serving my mother was priceless. I learned life lessons that could not be taught in class. She taught me how to deal with people, especially angry customers. But more importantly, she taught me how to generate and sell ideas to people. No one could have taught me better than she did. She generated business ideas, was running a successful business, and was always thinking about ways to expand.

The Unconventional Classrooms of Burkina Faso

School in Burkina Faso looks considerably different than in the United States. You may have realized this by now, just reading about my ability to work and sell food during 30-minute breaks. Not only that, but the number of students far exceeded the capacity of our schools and the number of teachers available.

Picture this: a single teacher attempting to guide 100-200 eager elementary students, each vying for a seat in the classroom that couldn't accommodate all. To cope with this overwhelming demand – half of the students would attend class in the morning while the rest lingered outside, awaiting their turn to learn in the afternoon. The classrooms were often basic and under-resourced, a stark contrast to what one might expect in more affluent countries. Desks and tables were scarce, often requiring students to share or, in some cases, sit on the floor due to the lack of furniture. The scarcity also extended to educational supplies; textbooks and writing materials were special commodities shared among students.

The challenge of hearing the teacher from the back of the room was significant. In a space crammed with 100-120 young elementary-aged students, the teacher's voice often struggled to reach the furthest corners, making it difficult for those seated at the back to follow the lesson. One had to have an incredible level of focus and determination to learn and succeed.

When present, the walls were sometimes made of mud bricks, with corrugated metal roofs that amplified the heat during the day, making the interior sweltering and uncomfortable. In some cases, classes were held outdoors under the shade of a tree, where the natural environment served as the classroom. This setting presented its own set of challenges with many more distractions.

High schools were even more crowded, and colleges were the worst places to learn, with about 3,000 students and only one professor. Class would begin at 7:00 a.m., but to get a good spot, you'd have to arrive by 4:00 a.m. Students often teamed up and took turns sleeping at the school to ensure they had a place in the classroom.

In these circumstances, teachers performed courageously, tasked with not only educating but also managing such a large group of young students and with limited resources. Their role extended beyond instruction; they were mentors, disciplinarians, and sometimes surrogate parents, providing guidance and care to their students.

This scenario, while challenging, also fostered a strong sense of community and resilience among students. They learned to support each other, sharing materials and knowledge and forming study groups to fill in the gaps left by the stretched educational system. The experience, though far from ideal, instilled in students a deep appreciation for education, a sense of resourcefulness, and an understanding of the value of collective effort and mutual support.

When the moment arrived for me to begin my formal education, my father had a clear vision in mind: for me to attend the Arabic School. Given his respected role as an imam within our community, this preference was deeply rooted in tradition and personal values. My father, an admirable religious leader, had himself mastered Arabic, the language of our faith, and saw it as a vital link to our cultural and spiritual heritage. He envisioned a future for me that mirrored his path, hoping I might one day step into his shoes and carry forward the legacy of spiritual leadership. His perspective was shaped by a profound respect for our traditions and the belief that learning Arabic would provide me with a direct connection to the rich theological and intellectual traditions of Islam.

However, all my siblings had attended French schools, making them well-versed in the language and culture that dominate our broader societal interactions. In contrast, my father saw in me the potential to blend both worlds: to uphold our spiritual and cultural roots through Arabic while fluently navigating the modern global landscape.

I wanted a different educational path. The pull towards the French school was strong, driven by both my personal interests and practical considerations. The French school represented a modern education, promising a curriculum that was both broad and adaptable to the world beyond our community. To me, it was not just about learning a language but embracing a platform that I believed would open up more opportunities—academic, professional, and personal.

While deeply respectful and understanding of my father's wishes for me to continue a legacy of religious scholarship and leadership, I also yearned for the diverse and comprehensive education that the French school offered. I saw it as a gateway to understanding the world in its plurality and complexity, equipping me with the tools to navigate and contribute to it effectively, possibly even within the sphere of spiritual leadership, but with a broader perspective.

The French school was highly regarded for its comprehensive curriculum and the quality of education it offered, making it a coveted choice for many students and parents alike. Beyond the prestige, the school promised more than just academic rigor; it was a path to broader opportunities, both locally and internationally. The French language, being a lingua franca in the realms of diplomacy, business, and academia, offered a significant advantage in the global landscape. Attending the French school meant not only gaining proficiency in a widely spoken language but also acquiring a set of skills and knowledge that would be invaluable in navigating future career paths and higher education opportunities.

I finally agreed with my father and attended the Arabic School for two years. As I got older, I knew I had to transition to the French school, or it would be too late. I begged and begged my father, but he was adamant that I was already in Arabic school, speaking Arabic, and well-known in the community.

Remember what I told you earlier about not taking no for an answer very well? So, I waited for my father to go to work and went to my uncle's house to ask him if he would register me for the French school. I told him my father said it was okay, and unfortunately, he forgot about taking me to school and went to work. I just needed my uncle to accompany me to the school and sign me up. Of course, he said "yes" because he thought my father had agreed to this. We went to school, put my name on the roster, and I was signed up for French School!

That evening, I returned home, showed my dad the registration documents I had signed up for, and asked for his acceptance once more. He said, "If you found a way to get there, that's your problem. You can figure it out!" And that's precisely what I did.

Entering the French school, they had wanted me to be in first grade because they thought I would be behind, as I had not spoken French. However, I was old enough to be in second or third, and I did not want to be behind. I knew that if I worked at it, I could catch up quickly and be at the same pace as the other kids my age. My older siblings had attended the French school, so I had heard enough to know what they were talking about.

I arrived at school early on the first day. I wanted to get there before the teacher to get a spot in the second-grade classroom, thinking they might not notice. Little did I know, being the new kid in school, that the other kids had specific "spots" where they liked to sit. Well, it turns out the spot I chose belonged to another boy, Issa, who was nicknamed "Bimbim" because he was big and well-built. He was not so happy when he walked in! With my stubborn personality, I didn't want to move and lose my seat, not only in the classroom but in the second grade. It didn't go over well with him, and just as the teacher arrived, Issa and I were rolling around on the ground fighting over the seat.

The teacher looked at me and said, "What are you doing in my classroom? I did not teach you in first grade; you should not be in here. And to top it off, you come into my classroom and start a fight. I do not want you here!"

I apologized and promised her that I would do well if she gave me another chance. She wasn't ready to believe me for she had no idea who I was, so she called in the principal. Thankfully, he knew my father when he arrived, so when I explained the situation, he agreed to give me a chance to stay in the second-grade classroom. I was on a trial period

– If I failed or did not do well, I would have to return to the first grade.

I was thankful and did not want to let the principal and the teacher down. I wanted to show them that I could not only pass but I could be at the top of the class. My elder brother Bouba was at the top of his class, so in the evenings, I asked him to help me with school, and by morning I would already know all the materials the teacher was to teach that day. I ended up being number one in my class within the first semester. However, because I was ahead and already well-versed in the material with Bouba's help, I would often get bored in class and give away the answers to the others. Let's just say I wasn't the teacher's favorite student.

I continued to excel in French school and was at the top of the class every year through primary school. When I was about to enter high school at age 12, my older brother, Madi, who had coached me throughout my schooling, fell ill with depression, which led to a serious mental illness. He was very sick and could no longer run his business. He knew I was good with sales and understood the basics of running a business because of my experience working with my mother and my kerosene venture with my grandmother.

Madi owned a small shop located conveniently close to our home and at the heart of our neighborhood where he sold a variety of items. It was essentially a mini grocery store. He had done so much for me, and I was excited at the chance to take another stab at running a business. Learning the ropes took a few weeks, but I quickly realized I could still go to high school and run the store if I hired another employee to oversee the company. While running my brother's business, I was introduced to some wealthier families in town. I wanted to expand the business, so I bought bread from the local bakery to deliver to families each morning. I built up my clientele to have about thirty local families to deliver bread to each morning!

As you'll find out later in this book, this bread route was the very business that aided in my chance to study in the United States and the entire reason I started Leading Change Africa.

My journey from the crowded classrooms of Burkina Faso to founding Leading Change Africa is a testament to the entrepreneurial spirit and leadership that have defined my path. Confronted with the realities of limited educational resources and the challenge of overcapacity in our schools, I learned early on the importance of resilience and perseverance. My determination to attend the French school, despite my father's expectations, and my venture into running a business while still in high school were my first real tests of initiative and resourcefulness. Adapting quickly to new environments and seizing opportunities for growth, such as expanding the business with a bread delivery service, highlighted a proactive approach to overcoming obstacles and pursuing success.

Engaging with my community and building a network through the business were pivotal steps to becoming a successful entrepreneur. By understanding and meeting the needs of local families, I helped grow my mother's business, expand my brother's store, and set the stage for my future endeavors. These experiences show the importance of building relationships and close community ties. Balancing the business demands with my education taught me how to think strategically and moreover, the value of having a clear vision, even when faced with challenges.

Ultimately, my story is one of transformation, shaped by the values of leadership and entrepreneurship. From overcoming the challenges of my youth in Burkina Faso to founding Leading Change Africa, each step has been guided by a strong vision and a deep commitment to giving back. This journey has and continues to shape me as a leader and a person. My experiences remind me how personal achievements can be leveraged for broader societal change, embodying what it means to lead and innovate for the greater good — not just for personal gain.

As you reflect on your own path, consider how your unique experiences and challenges have equipped you with the resilience, insight, and creativity to lead and innovate. Remember, true leadership is not measured by the heights we reach alone but by our ability to lift others as we rise. Let this be a reminder that each of us holds the potential to affect meaningful change, driven by a vision that extends beyond ourselves to the wider community and world we are a part of. How will you harness your journey to inspire and enact change for the greater good?

"It's about moving forward without placing blame…"

2

Crossing Continents for a Dream

I continued to support my brother with his business, hiring more employees to help with day-to-day operations while I juggled my bread delivery business and attended high school. It was around this same time that my father had passed away. I remember that day vividly as if it were yesterday. Before I left that morning, I visited him in his room. He grabbed my hand longer than usual, put his right hand on my head and said blessing after blessing silently.

My heart was heavy when I left him and went to school. I am usually enthusiastic and dynamic in school, but that day, I was particularly sad and silent. Around 11:00 am, my teacher called me out and said that the school principal wanted to talk to me. I went to the office, and he said that I should go home. At that time, I knew something had happened at home while I was in school.

When I arrived home, the main room was crowded with family, and my dad was covered, lying on the floor in the middle of the main room. I removed the cloth that had covered him slightly to look at his face for the last time. I could not help the tears running down my face. I cried and cried.

It was very, very hard for me. I looked up to my father, and I wanted him to live long to see me succeed and repay him for everything he did for me. Reflecting on this death, we could not figure out why he had been sick for almost two years. We went to several hospitals and would never get a clear answer. We would revert to traditional medicine, then back to modern, and still, no solution.

Some say that he had recurring misunderstandings and fights with other religious leaders, and a curse or something mystical must have happened to him. We decided to leave his death a mystery and honor his time with us on earth as an incredible father, leader, and husband.

Through all this, my mother continued to be the strongest woman I knew, running a successful business, raising children, and caring for the house. I didn't know it then, but looking back, I acknowledge her as the force behind my resilience, determination, and endless pursuit of knowledge and personal growth.

I never saw our need for more money as a limitation. I always believed that you could only grow within your means and continue to aim higher from there. Instead of viewing challenges as setbacks, I've learned to view them as opportunities; the only way from here is up. It's about moving forward without placing blame, realizing it's just part of the journey.

I committed to myself that I would continue to strive for excellence and be at the top of my class so that I could attend school abroad. It wasn't just about escaping the challenges in my community; instead, it was a determination to uncover the secrets of the developing nations and bring back these ideas for my people. I firmly believed there was a vast world brimming with insight, experiences, and untapped solutions – and that quality education was a driving force behind it all. My vision was to equip myself with the knowledge and tools to break down barriers and improve the situation of my own people. I dreamed of a more accessible and fair education system for the youth in my country.

A turning point came during late-night adventures with a wealthy friend, Aziz. Aziz's father was a doctor, and his mother worked for a major company. Since Aziz did not have to work to pay for his education, he often found himself with a lot of spare time. He would spend most of his free time playing video games and exploring other technology. On nights that I didn't feel like sleeping, I would close my store at midnight and head over to his house to play video games with him.

One evening, he asked me to go to a Cyber Café with him. He told me that there were machines where you could talk to anyone in the world. In complete awe, I didn't hesitate one bit. Although skeptical at first, Aziz guided me, and I messaged someone in Paris and instantly received a message back from him. I was in complete shock. Realizing its potential for research, Aziz knew exactly what I was thinking and nodded affirmatively, setting my plans in motion.

Over the next several weeks, I immersed myself in the Cyber Café. I knew that my ticket to the United States depended on learning how to use the internet. I needed to teach myself the fundamentals. The very next morning, I did my usual routine: wake up at 4 am, bike to the bakery, serve my clients, wake up my brother to watch the store for me so I could attend my classes, and return to relieve him. However, I asked my brother to cover my shift for another 2 hours that day.

I wasted my first two hours clicking and looking everywhere. Since I didn't know how to type, I didn't know how to find the keys quickly. Combining a slow internet with all of that, I spent extra time accessing a particular website. After countless hours at the café and much trial and error, I could finally do the same basics as Aziz. I started to use correspondence websites to communicate with strangers around the world. I was focused on finding friends from Canada and the U.S., but I did not have much luck finding correspondents in the U.S. I sent friend requests and got some responses. I was excited and kept exchanging messages with my new virtual friends. We stayed connected for a while.

After learning how to communicate with others and how to write an email correctly, I wondered what else the computer could do. I entered keywords in Google and quickly learned that I could research and learn about anything. Because of my longtime dream of studying in the U.S., I quickly looked for universities and colleges. I used Google to find a particular website, and then went back to Google to translate the language on the university's website if they did not have a French version. My research went faster after attending a U.S. embassy workshop where the presenter recommended specific websites to make my research easier. I eventually created a sound plan to study in the U.S.

The United States has some of the most prestigious Universities, more advanced facilities and resources, endless employment opportunities, and diverse cultures with students from around the world.

People often ask me, "Why Wisconsin?" Well, I typed in "Best University to study," and the University of Wisconsin - Madison happened to be in the top 20 for their business school. Red was my favorite color, and so that was the one I chose. My mind was made up; I just needed to find a way to get there.

I decided to ask the six families on my bread delivery route for help. I went door to door, explaining my plan and asking if they would help pay for my trip to Wisconsin and provide for my education if I was to be accepted into college. I got five no's before one kind woman, Mrs. Ouedraogo, said yes!

She said, *"I don't know you very well, but you bring me bread every morning, and I can see that you work hard."*

She took a chance on me. Now, it was up to me to figure out the rest and ensure I did not disappoint her.

Since we had only just begun learning basic English in high school, my English was very broken, making the process more challenging. I would have to use my friend's computer to translate all communication with the school from English to French as we communicated back and forth. I had everything set up to attend school in the United States and was excited!

When it was time to get my visa, the man working at the counter asked me if I knew where I was heading. He said, *"You know it snows over there?"* I said *"yes,"* I was excited (little did I know what I was getting myself into!)

The plan was for me to first attend WESLI, the Wisconsin English as a Second Language Institute, then apply for the local community College, and eventually attend the University of Wisconsin-Madison. WESLI offers individualized teaching, small class sizes, and a diverse student population. You can learn the English language, immerse yourself in a new culture, and equip yourself with the tools to attend college.

But before we get into that, my trip to the United States was nothing short of an adventure.

The Girl at the Airport

Finally, the moment I had been waiting for arrived as I boarded the airplane bound for Wisconsin, one step closer to making my dream a reality. I was 21 years old, having left my family behind to chase after the dreams of my youth. The overwhelming emotions brought tears to my eyes, for I could not believe it was actually happening.

I was to fly from Burkina Faso to Paris, Paris to Detroit, and Detroit to Wisconsin. This was not only my first time on a plane but also my first time leaving Africa. The flight from Burkina Faso to Paris was long, and I eventually fell asleep. When a flight attendant woke me up to offer a meal, I turned it down because the food seemed strange to me.

Once we landed in Paris, I had a one-day layover.

During this time, I met Amadou, a guy from Cameroon who spoke French and was on the same flight to the US for a conference. We had lunch, and he shared valuable advice about what I could expect in the United States since he had spent some time here studying in college.

Amadou and I then flew to Detroit, Michigan, where we said goodbye. He gave me his phone number and encouraged me to reach out later. I waited at the airport for my connecting flight to Wisconsin but soon realized my flight had been canceled. Now, here I was in the U.S., barely speaking English, and just had my flight canceled.

Panic started to set in. I was wondering how I would make it to Wisconsin on time as I had arranged for a representative from the school to welcome me at the airport in Madison to take me to the residential hall. I decided to call the school number I was given and tell them about the situation.

However, I did not know how to use the pay phone at the airport and needed help. Barely speaking English, I looked around for someone who might be able to help me.

I saw a girl sitting looking at her computer screen,

seeming busy, and a guy sitting silently eating his sandwich. I decided to interrupt the girl, for I had experienced that women are often kinder than men. This judgment proved to be true.

Fortunately, even with my poor English and awkward hand gestures, she knew what I was trying to say. Her name was Amanda, my first American friend. She took me to the pay phone, where I handed her my credit card and phone number so she could help make the phone call. After multiple failed attempts and a lot of anxiety on my end, we realized I hadn't activated my credit card yet.

Amanda asked me where I was trying to call. I showed her the number. After recognizing it was a U.S. phone number, she offered to make the call on her phone. My face brightened again. Amanda made multiple phone calls with no luck. It was already late, and there was no one in the office. She assured me not to worry after seeing the fear in my eyes and panic in my voice. She said she was taking the same flight to Wisconsin to see her boyfriend, Duc, and promised to make another call when we arrived.

I did not want to lose sight of her because she was my only chance at reaching my final destination, WESLI. We flew to Madison on a small airplane. Amanda sat a few rows behind me, so I was reassured I would not lose sight of her when the flight landed in Wisconsin.

When the flight finally touched down, Amanda made another phone call to the university. No one picked up the phone, and no one at the airport was waiting to welcome me. Amanda promised to make sure I got to where I needed to be. She explained the situation to her boyfriend, Duc, who had come to welcome her at the airport.

Duc had moved to Wisconsin from Texas to complete his Master's and Ph.D. degrees in nuclear engineering. I have met kind people in my life, but Duc was exceptional. He offered to give me a ride and let me stay in his one-bedroom apartment that night until we could reach someone at WESLI the next day during business hours. Exhausted from the previous night's travels, I slept soundly on the warm bed that Amanda had prepared on the floor for me.

The following day, Amanda treated me to a delicious American breakfast of omelets and pancakes, food I had never eaten before. I loved it. Later that day, eager to introduce me to more American cuisine, Amanda and Duc took me to a local pizza place in Madison, Ian's Pizza, for my first-ever taste of a staple college food – pizza! I chose the Macaroni and Cheese combination. It brought back memories of my grandma's delicious homemade comfort food; after tasting it, I would take off my shoes and wiggle my toes. I almost did the same at the restaurant. For dinner that evening, we explored another classic American restaurant, Olive Garden, which has since become one of my favorite go-to restaurants in the States.

Tackled the Chicken First

Among the whirlwind of adjustments and cultural shifts I encountered upon my arrival—from the open displays of affection to the wide variety of American cuisine—the experience at an 'all-you-can-eat' buffet with Amanda and Duc notably stood out. This was not merely an introduction to a new dining concept; it was symbolic of the vast array of choices and freedoms that define American life, mirroring the adaptability and decision-making I was rapidly learning to navigate.

As I walked into the restaurant, my eyes widened in amazement at the endless options available. Each dish's unique flavors and ingredients represented a world of possibilities, much like my journey to the U.S., This buffet taught me a valuable lesson in prioritization—choosing what mattered most from a seemingly infinite menu of life's opportunities. It wasn't feasible to sample every dish on the buffet, just as it wasn't possible to seize every opportunity before me. This realization struck a chord, emphasizing the importance of making informed choices and focusing on what truly mattered for my future — my big vision.

This lesson at the buffet was a reflection on American culture's emphasis on individual choice and personal freedom. Back in Burkina Faso, decisions are often made within the context of community and family needs. In contrast, here in America, the buffet—and, by extension, life itself—offered a canvas of personal choice, celebrated and encouraged in all its forms. This day at the restaurant with Amanda and Duc was an enlightening experience that shaped my understanding of autonomy and self-direction, integral to my growth as a leader and entrepreneur.

My arrival to the Unites States in the fall introduced me to the changing seasons, each bearing its own lessons. Unlike those who have grown accustomed to these shifts, I found profound wisdom in the cycle of change, embracing the adaptability required to navigate new challenges. The first snowfall, magical at first, soon revealed the harsh cold that accompanied it. Yet, instead of yielding to discomfort, I sought ways to thrive, embodying the lesson that change is constant and adaptation is key.

As Jim Rohn wisely stated, *"We cannot change the seasons, but we can change ourselves."* The harsh Wisconsin winter didn't just test my resilience against the cold; it mirrored the broader journey of personal growth, teaching me to embrace each season's unique lessons. With its promise of renewal, spring encouraged me to seize opportunities and nurture new ideas and relationships. Summer taught me the importance of guarding my values and efforts against external threats. And as fall arrived again, it brought a time of harvest, a reminder to take ownership of my efforts and outcomes without reservation.

Each first season in Wisconsin was a chapter in my own story of resilience, growth, and personal accountability.

"It wasn't about the money. Instead, it was about...taking a chance on others."

3

Paying It Forward for Global Change: The Power of Vision and Mentorship

In the previous chapter, I shared the reason I was able to come to study in the United States: one kind woman, Mrs. Ouedraogo, took a chance on me. It was because of her financial help that I could pursue my dreams of studying in the United States – opening my eyes to the limitless opportunities and potential to help my own country, Burkina Faso.

I always wondered why this woman helped me. I spent months trying to figure out how I would ever repay her the money she lent me to make this all a reality. But in time, she helped me realize that it wasn't about the money. Instead, it was about paying it forward and taking a chance on others.

With Amanda and Duc's help, I connected with the

WESLI staff and settled into the student's residence hall, where I would stay for the next four months. WESLI provided a bridge between one's home country and the United States, easing the cultural transition for many international students—the program aimed to enhance English proficiency and helped students navigate the nuances of American culture.

Because someone else was sponsoring my education, and I didn't have much money, I only spent about four months at WESLI before transferring to Madison College. The typical student stayed a minimum of six months. I studied every chance I got and engrossed myself in every program they offered. In addition to the intensive English program at WESLI, Amanda and Duc helped me with grammar and vocabulary lessons on the side. With their guidance, I eagerly prepared for the next phase of my education at Madison College.

After successfully completing the program at WESLI, I went on to receive my associate's degree from Madison College.

After the first full-time semester, my GPA was 4.0. This academic standing qualified me for the Phi Theta Kappa International Honor Society membership.

In high school, I was involved in student organizations and learned that leadership development is a daily process in educational classroom settings and through community involvement. I then decided to volunteer at the Madison Children's Museum. I loved it. I was allocating my idle time to an organization that needed it the most, plus I enjoyed playing with the kids. These young kids brightened my days with their smiles and helped me quickly improve my English skills. Some of them found my African accent funny and often tried to imitate it. They made me laugh all the time. I sometimes returned to college with stories to tell.

In school, I was also learning about inclusiveness, advocacy, and stewardship, and I later campaigned for a Student Ambassador position and a Student Senate seat. My four-semester journey went from Senator to Vice-President of Communications to Senate President. Two years later, I was selected as the Wisconsin Technical Colleges System State Ambassador, a position that represents over 400,000 students. I was the first African and black person to be elected student body president and could not believe that a delivery boy from Africa could represent an entire state. I seized the opportunity to volunteer and made lasting relationships that still serve me well today.

I ultimately completed my Associate Degree in Science at Madison College, transferred to the University of Wisconsin-Madison (UW-Madison) to complete my bachelor's degree. I was fortunate enough to be selected as the Jack Kent Cooke Foundation (JKCF) Transfer Scholar. The JKCF Scholarship is the largest private Scholarship in the United States, providing up to $40,000 every year for three years to community college students whose school nominates them based on several factors, including academic excellence and financial need.

Like most of my fellow JKCF Scholars, who are committed to promoting valuable qualities and serving their fellow students, my passion led me one more time to run for office during my first semester at UW-Madison to serve my peers and bring about change on campus. I was selected as the Associated Student of Madison Shared Governance Policy Director and was elected the following year to represent the university in two capacities: Business School Student Council Representative and Student Services Finance Committee Representative. I was again given the opportunity to represent a student population of about 42,000 people and manage segregated fees of over $32 million. It was both a privilege and an honor for me.

Through extracurricular activities such as the African Student Association, Student Government, and Student Ambassador Program, I have met numerous people who share my interest in making the world a better place for everyone. They all wanted a safe and inclusive environment, a good education, and the skills to succeed in a highly competitive job market. However, most of them were from countries with adequate educational systems. Students from Western Europe, the United States, or Japan do not have to envision better educational settings.

As you know, I left my country, Burkina Faso (BF), to pursue a better education than my home country could provide. There are only three major universities in the entire country, and students do not get to choose their career interests. There is also an overcrowding of students and inaccessibility to certain classes. The class size can range from 2000 to 3000 students, with one professor using a microphone.

Having had the opportunity to experience a different academic setting, I wanted to contribute to improving the educational system in my home country. I wanted to make a difference not only for the development of my people but also for the sake of a continent that still lacks developmental strategies.

During this time, I enrolled in The Accenture Leadership Center (ALC), the go-to place that offers students unique, hands-on opportunities to develop leadership skills during their undergraduate careers. The ALC enables students to develop and hone their leadership skills and gain experience and knowledge to help them excel in classes, extracurricular activities, and future careers.

I was specifically enrolled in a six-day leadership boot camp, for lack of a better term. This camp took place off-campus in Oconomowoc, Wisconsin. There were 65 eager University students ready to learn. The week's theme was learning to lead with integrity, and our big assignment was to create a vision. We were to find something we were passionate about and create that vision. We were given an oversized post-it note to help explain our vision for the group. Some drew elaborate pictures, some wrote bullet points, and some wrote paragraphs — whatever worked for them.

This was the first time I wrote my vision down on paper for Leading Change Africa on paper. We went around the room, and each individual shared their vision and the story behind it. I shared my journey to the United States and my life back in my home country, Burkina Faso, Africa. I wanted to improve the educational system in Burkina Faso and bring about positive change for the entire continent of Africa by developing leaders and change agents.

When I shared my vision, I could see that the others in the room could see it, too. I knew I had an idea I needed to hang on to. At the end of the day, the Lead Facilitator, John Leffin, approached me and said, *"Ousmane, this is possible; reach out to me later."*

John was a leading Partner at Accenture, one of the world's largest global consulting firms, and played a part in developing The Accenture Leadership Center at the University School of Business for the University of Wisconsin - Madison. John was committed to shaping the future of leaders and continues to impact my life significantly and the success of Leading Change Africa.

Retiring at a young age, John has been able to spend the last 20 years dedicated to coaching and mentoring the next generation of leaders. His vision is to be a catalyst for positive growth in the lives of others. John and his wife Loretta started the Leffin Family Foundation, where they focus on giving back to high-impact organizations that focus primarily on education and meet three specific goals. They choose organizations in which they believe:

1. In their VISION
2. In their leadership's ability to achieve the vision
3. In the organization's operational excellence — they will steward the money well and it won't be wasted.

I contacted John and went to coffee with him to share more about my background and vision for Leading Change Africa. John and his wife had a scholarship program for a Master's in Accounting and Finance. I received the scholarship and landed a position at Ernst & Young, where I worked full-time for three years.

Over those next three years, I continued to work on bringing my vision of the organization to life. I asked John Leffin to mentor me along the way. Near the end of the third year at Ernst & Young, I told John I was considering leaving the company to devote full-time to Leading Change Africa.

I'm unsure if these were his exact words, but John told me this was a terrible idea. He wasn't against me putting more time and energy behind the organization, but he was worried that I was leaving a steady paycheck and a network of people who had money that could help to fund Leading Change Africa. He was concerned that I would lose my platform and potential funding sources.

Although his points were all very valid, I knew in my heart that I needed to do this. I decided to take the leap of faith and quit my steady job at Ernst and Young to pursue Leading Change Africa full-time. To take Africa to a whole new level, I needed to create jobs along the way. It would be a considerable risk, but if it didn't work or if I was unsuccessful, I'd still have learned a lot of other skills that would help in my life.

I believe that we have to BE THE CHANGE we want to see! If you don't like what you see, don't let someone else take the lead. Be part of the change you want to see and take leadership.

What bothers you? What makes you mad? What keeps you up at night? How can you change that?

For many of the Scholars in Burkina Faso, their problems were significant, *"I don't have electricity, and I want to solve that."* Or, *"I don't have water and want to find ways to bring it back to my community."*

Education, entrepreneurship, and change are the three core areas that are critical to one's success. When I say education, I'm not necessarily talking about getting a Ph.D. or even a Master's degree; rather, what are you always doing to improve yourself as you move forward? What are you reading, and what people are you surrounding yourself with so that you're continuing to grow? If you're not growing and challenging yourself, you're actually shrinking. In life, you either move upward or downwards; you can not stay still. We see millionaires who haven't finished their education - but have educated themselves along the way, adopted an entrepreneurial mindset, and embraced change, becoming wildly successful.

Before I continue, let's return to my mentor, John, and my last day at Ernst & Young. After much discussion, John gave me his blessing, and I reached out to my boss, David Gay's assistant, to coordinate a breakfast meeting with him as we often did. The goal was to share with him my plans of leaving his firm and also ask for his blessings.

When I shared the news, he mentioned that he was not surprised that I would make such a decision and that over my time at his firm, he was expecting such a decision at some point. We had an enjoyable time, and he proceeded to give me one last piece of advice: *"You have a lot of potential and great strengths, and as you are starting on your own, recognize that just like everyone else, you will identify your weaknesses. Don't be discouraged when you do. Just make sure to hire competent and smart people to compensate for your areas of weakness."*

To this day, I haven't forgotten that advice, and every time I am with my intelligent and capable team members, I think of my previous boss. Over time, and as I continued to reflect on his words of wisdom, I learned not to be upset if I found out that I showed weakness in some areas. I am happy that I found my limitations because knowing them and dealing with them will increase my chances of improving and moving forward towards achieving my goals.

If I am disappointed because I can't be the best person to do everything myself, I am terribly naive and certainly haven't learned the lessons my boss was trying to teach me. So, I forgive myself for my weaknesses and recognize that nobody can do everything well. I wouldn't want my best-skilled surgeon to be on my favorite soccer team if he can't kick a ball like a real professional player, and I am sure you wouldn't want that, either. In listening to David and going back to reflect on my own weaknesses, I realized that I have three choices:

1. I can deny them, which is what most of us do;
2. I can accept them and work at them to try to convert them into strengths. That might or might not work depending on my willingness to put in the effort and my ability to change.
3. I can accept my weaknesses and find ways around them.

In all three cases, the solution I choose will be critically important to the direction of my life. The worst path I could take is to deny my weaknesses. When it comes to business, asking others who are strong to help us in areas where we are weak to help us is a great skill that we should develop no matter what. It will assist us in creating a system that will prevent us from doing what we shouldn't be doing in the first place. All successful people are good at this. My old boss is no doubt successful!

Following David's invaluable advice, and embracing my team's strength, I came to another critical understanding—one that extended beyond accepting my weaknesses and leveraging connections effectively.

David had generously shared not only his wisdom but also his contact details, ensuring I could reach out whenever needed. However, apart from sending wishes on special occasions, I learned an essential strategy for initiating more formal interactions, like arranging our meetings. I didn't grasp this approach immediately but discovered it through a blend of persistence and insight.

The realization came after an event that marked a turning point in my networking strategy. Attending a significant fundraiser, I had the chance to meet a businessman I had long admired, facilitated by an introduction from a partner at EY. Unlike my earlier, more direct attempts at networking, this encounter was strategic and mindful. The businessman, appreciating the respect and discretion shown, shared his direct contact information with me, a gesture of trust and openness.

However, the true lesson emerged when I attempted to schedule a follow-up meeting. Initially, I thought direct contact was the best approach, but experience taught me otherwise. Successful individuals often delegate the management of their business calendar to their executive assistants—a role of critical importance and trust. Understanding this, I realized that reaching out to the executive assistant was not just practical; it was a sign of respect for the executive's time and priorities.

By acknowledging the executive assistant's significant role and addressing them with the respect their position commands, I found a more effective path to securing meetings. This strategy wasn't about bypassing the direct line to the executive but respecting their time and the organizational structure they'd put in place. It reinforced a fundamental lesson: recognizing and valuing the roles of all team members, from CEOs to executive assistants, is crucial in the business world. So, for any aspiring leader or entrepreneur looking to connect with industry giants, remember the power of strategic follow-up and the importance of respecting those who manage the gates to influential figures.

Harnessing the advice from David to embrace my weaknesses and seek support from those who have been on the path before, I continued to build and nurture the new influential relationships I have formed in the United States.

As I mentioned before, John was one that I went to often. After leaving Ernst & Young to pursue Leading Change Africa full-time, I would meet with John once per month, whether we went for coffee, talked on the phone, or met via Zoom. I made sure to come to the meeting prepared with an agenda, for I knew his time was valuable, and I was grateful for the wisdom and knowledge he would share with me. I also believe that one of the reasons I have made it this far is my willingness and desire to always continue learning. At the end of each of our sessions, I still ask:

1. What are you reading?
2. What piece of advice do you have for me today?

John has provided invaluable financial support to the organization and connected me with some of the most influential people who continue to shape Leading Change Africa today. Because of his successful career at one of the largest global consulting firms, John was connected to many intelligent, influential people in the community. He served on several nonprofit boards, spent 15+ years working in Haiti, and started his own family foundation to continue giving back and making a more significant impact on the causes he cared about most.

He introduced me to Dale Dawson, founder and CEO of Bridge to Rwanda. John saw the successful model that Dale had built his organization on and thought it would be a perfect fit for Leading Change Africa.

Not only would it set the organization up with a more sustainable financial model, but it would also expand the number of students we could impact.

John shared, *"The challenge we've always faced in Haiti is that you help educate Haitians, and many of them want to leave and get opportunities elsewhere, which is understandable; however, if all these highly educated people leave Haiti, how are you going to change the country? You need to build opportunities and the desire for people to stay right where they're at so they can be the new leaders, and that's a big part of Ousmane's vision, which resembles that of Bridge to Rwanda. And that's how you change a country. Sending kids to college is great, but if you send a bunch of Scholars to the US and they never go back, you won't change the country."*

In the next couple of chapters of this book, you'll learn more about the requirements for our Scholars of Leading Change Africa, but this idea has been a driving factor for how we will create change in Africa for years to come.

John continues to connect me with key people in my journey, and I will forever be grateful for his guidance and support.

"The task of securing funding ... was daunting... I knew I had to figure it out."

4

Breakfast Meetings

During one of my MBA classes, a man by the name of Steve Wallman came in to give a presentation about business, entrepreneurship, and investment. Steve previously worked at Merryl Lynch, a large investment firm, before creating his own successful firm, Wallman Investment. He helped bring our very first Scholar to the United States and continues to be a mentor and friend to me to this day.

It seemed as though everyone in the class was nodding off to Steve's presentation, but there was something about him that kept me at the edge of my seat the entire time. When his presentation was over, and class was dismissed, I quickly grabbed my backpack and ran down the hall to catch Steve before he'd left.

I told him how I enjoyed his speech and shared my vision for creating Leading Change Africa. I asked him if he would consider having coffee with me so I could ask him a few questions and seek his advice.

Wallman agreed, and a few days later, we met for coffee. I've always been an avid note-taker, because it allows me to internalize the conversation and go back when I need to gain clarity. I had a small Moleskine journal where I would write down every important idea I heard. I wanted to take in as much of his knowledge and information as I possibly could.

Steve said, *"I've talked to many journalists over the years, and I don't think I've ever had anyone write down what I was saying with as much intensity as Ousmane did. So that automatically singles him out as someone unique."*

Steve and I hit it off, and he continues to be a mentor for me and a driving force for Leading Change Africa.

When I first shared my idea and vision with Steve, he had two distinct ideas or nuggets of wisdom for me to consider.

    1. Having been In the investment business, Steve

shared that the goal is always to double your money. It's an amazing success when you get to 10 doubles in the investment business. If you find an investment that doubles ten times in size, value, and scope, it's a huge winner. It's 1000x gain. In this case, instead of doubling the money, it would be a great way to think about how we bring in Scholars at Leading Change Africa — we'd go from 1 to 2 to 4 to 8 and so on. So that's where the idea of influencing 1024 Scholars came from (that's ten doubles). The current vision of Leading Change Africa is to transform 1,024 Young Africans into leaders and leaders into agents of change by 2030 and directly and indirectly impact 1 million individuals by 2050.

2. The other idea we discussed is paying it forward. Years earlier, when Steve was starting out, he had a difficult time finding people who would lend a hand or piece of advice. He promised himself that he wouldn't be as arrogant as the people he encountered on the way up. As long as it aligns with his values, Steve is willing to help those who ask for it. So, when I came to him to ask him to help students from Burkina Faso try to do what I did — to come to the United States, learn English, enroll in the local Technical College, work hard, and earn a

scholarship to complete their education — he said yes...

On one condition: The students who are funded have to pay it forward to at least two others. The idea was that if you received a scholarship, you had to promise you'd help two other people do what you did. We didn't give guidelines about when or how it had to be done; they just promised they would. My entire vision behind the organization was always to pay it forward to others in the same way I was given the chance to come to the United States by Mrs. Ouedraogo.

Steve shares, *"Entrepreneurs succeed against all odds. In the end, the one ingredient every successful entrepreneur has is this incredible drive that overcomes every obstacle in its path. Almost every entrepreneur who succeeds has had moments where failure was imminent, certain, minutes away, that kind of thing — but they're able to overcome it and continue moving forward.*

I believe that the effects of Leading Change Africa will be better than almost all scholarship programs because of the ripple effect it will create."

Steve provided the first scholarship for a young man

named Adama to come to the United States. Since then, he's continued to support both behind the scenes as a mentor and financially to ensure the sustained success of Leading Change so that we can continue to help more young Africans realize their potential and chase their dreams of changing the trajectory of their communities.

Without Steve's support, we would not be where we are today.

On a Mission to Forge a Future of Renewable Energy in Africa

From the heart of rural Burkina Faso, as the third of nine siblings, unfolds a narrative of aspiration and resilience in the face of generational barriers and financial constraints. Adama's parents, whose education finished before the completion of middle school, set the stage of challenges and limited opportunities. Yet, it was Adama's discovery of Leading Change Africa that marked the beginning of a new chapter in his life. Upon encountering the application, Adama saw a glimpse of hope, stating, *"I saw an opportunity to break my family and myself out of the poverty cycle. It was my chance to help people in the same shoes as I was, live a better life, and change the future for our community."*

Chosen as the first Scholar of the Leading Change Africa program, Adama's academic efforts led him to Madison College, where he pursued and earned his Associate Degree, setting his sights on a Bachelor of Science in Electrical Engineering. His tenure as an intern at Alliant Energy further cemented his commitment to renewable energy, a field he had been passionate about from early on. Leading Change Africa played a pivotal role in shaping his vision, offering programs that extend beyond conventional education to include real-world skills in financial literacy, personal development, teamwork, and leadership.

The significance of Adama's journey is also deeply rooted in the community and experiences facilitated by Leading Change Africa, which served as a source of inspiration and positive reinforcement. These interactions have highlighted the importance of community service and the power of connecting with mentors and peers, demonstrating the possibilities of creating change within one's community.

With aspirations to start his own business in Africa, Adama aims to leverage his education and experiences to make a significant impact. He articulates his gratitude and future intentions, saying, *"Thank you for touching my life and helping lift up many people directly and indirectly out of poverty, giving them a chance to make the best of themselves. I'd like to reassure you that your generosity will be reciprocated with hard work, dedication, and a true commitment to bring the fruits of what you've sewn. In that way, we can show our gratitude, but for now, thank you."*

Turning a vision into reality requires identifying opportunities, building connections, and being open to guidance from those who have walked the path before. My interactions with John, Steve, David, and so many more have helped lay the groundwork for the impactful work we do at Leading Change Africa. Their willingness to share their experience, wisdom, and ways to overcome challenges continues to guide me in making decisions for the organization today. I've learned that mentorship is an ongoing process, with each interaction offering valuable insights for moving forward.

As you consider the narratives shared in this chapter, think about the mentors in your own life—those who have shared their knowledge and experiences to guide you. Mentorship is more than just receiving advice; it's a reciprocal relationship that encourages mutual development, challenges our thinking, and helps us advance toward our objectives. Let this serve as a reminder that you, too, have the capacity to be a mentor to others as you learn and grow as a leader. How will you engage in mentorship, both as a contributor and beneficiary of shared knowledge, to create a legacy of growth and positive change?

"Almost every entrepreneur who succeeds has had moments where failure was imminent..."

5

Partnerships, Collaborations, and Strategic Decisions

Lara and her partner Grant, both dedicated parents, lawyers, and active community members, had their lives forever changed when a friend passed by their house.

In 2018, Lara stood in the front yard as their friend John drove past. He rolled down his window and said, *"We have one student coming from Burkina Faso. Will you let him come live with you?"*

And without much hesitation, she said, *"Sure, why not? That sounds fun!"* Lara and Grant had both been active in the Peace Corps, had lived in Africa, and knew there were incredible human beings who could benefit from their support and mentorship.

One Scholar turned into two, and they welcomed Onesime Zongo and Ousmane Nikiema.

Lara shares, *"They are extraordinary human beings. I was immediately struck by their joy to be and their dedication to their own self-growth and their country. Particularly in today's times, things can get really dark and feel very hopeless, and yet their eyes were full of hope."*

Lara and her family embraced Onesime and Ousmane, providing them a home to live in and the support to succeed. From navigating the challenges of transferring schools to offering direction on student loans and guidance with cultural transitions, Lara and her family became an integral part of their lives.

Simple things we often take for granted in a more developed country, like learning to swim, driving a car, and picking apples, were things they had never before experienced, and now they could.

Lara's dedication to the Scholars and Leading Change Africa led her to become an active member of the President's Council. She continues to share the mission and vision of the organization — and we are incredibly grateful for her work.

"The energy, creativity, and the hope that Leading Change embodies is next level. *I have been on other boards and other public interest committees, focusing on social justice, and the immediacy with which I wanted to get involved with this organization stands in stark contrast to other experiences!*

Ousmane Kabre has a way in which he truly sees you and values you. He wants you to come along and be part of this incredible mission. He sees you making an impact. And most importantly, ***every single one of the Scholars fully embodies what the mission of the organization is all about — igniting hope and change.*** *They exude it, and make you want to be a part of it,"* said Lara.

Lara believes, as I do, that *"any funds given to Leading Change Africa are going to really deserving and incredible human beings. These kids are fantastic and deserve every bit of support we can give them. They will NOT take it for granted. They will use it to the best of their ability and in ways that I think everyone would be proud of."*

Lara's story is a testament to the profound impact that the organization has on the lives of these young individuals. It's also a testament to the critical importance of collaboration and mentorship both for the success of individuals and organizations.

Lara was connected to me by my mentor, John Leffin, who you learned about earlier in the book. It's critical to recognize that many of my initial connections evolved into meaningful partnerships and have aided in the growth and success of the organization.

The initial President's Council was made up of 12 members. Collaborating with like-minded individuals who shared our vision allowed us to leverage diverse expertise and resources, encouraging innovation and scalability. Through these partnerships, we gained access to valuable networks, funding opportunities, and strategic insights that moved our mission forward. By bringing together a group of successful individuals from various backgrounds and industries, we had a wealth of experience, perspectives, and resources at the table, enabling us to make more informed decisions and navigate difficult challenges more effectively.

The President's Council continues to serve as a pillar of leadership within our organization, providing me guidance, mentorship, and accountability as the leader of Leading Change Africa. Interacting with this group has been instrumental in the organization's growth and my personal growth as a leader, allowing me to learn from their experiences, perspectives, and leadership styles.

Their collective wisdom has helped me develop strategic thinking, effective communication skills, and the ability to inspire and motivate others toward our shared vision.

Adapting and Overcoming: Strategic Leadership in Uncertain Times

I would be remiss if I didn't share the challenges of the pandemic in 2020, as we all know as Covid-19. Leading Change Africa was still a very young organization, so it may come as no surprise that we quickly had to pivot when COVID-19 hit in March of 2020 and everything shut down. "Pivot" became the word used by many businesses, people, and non-profit organizations. We could no longer bring students to the United States, not to mention the parents of the Scholars who were already in the program were worried.

It felt as though the weight of the world was on my shoulders. Right before the pandemic, we had just selected a cohort of twelve Scholars coming to the United States and Rwanda for our program. However, because travel was shut down, everything stopped. As I mentioned, the parents weren't only worried about their children but also counted on me to ensure that I still delivered on my promise. They didn't want their kids to wait another year to start their education.

This was a big deal for the parents. Not only was it a difficult decision to allow their children to leave the country and trust me with them. Most students do very well here, but like normal humans, some make mistakes along the way. The Scholars become like family to me because I am their go-to confidant in their journey. It was a significant responsibility to take on, especially when I was still so young myself.

I needed to ensure that I could fulfill the promise I had made to the families and the Scholars and find the funding to cover their education and program expenses. It was a huge burden, but I knew I had to figure it out. I remember feeling an overwhelming mix of determination and pressure. Knowing that the trust of these families and the futures of these Scholars rested on my shoulders added a weighted sense of responsibility. It was a challenge that kept me awake many nights, pondering solutions and strategies. Despite my youth, I understood the magnitude of what I had committed to and the impact it would have not only on the students' lives but also on their families back home. This was not just about providing an education; it was about changing lives and potentially the trajectory of entire communities.

The task of securing funding for their education and program expenses was daunting. Yet, with every challenge, my resolve to succeed only strengthened. I recognized that these Scholars represented hope— a hope for a better future for themselves and for their families. As their confidant and mentor, I became deeply invested in their success and well-being, feeling a profound sense of duty to uphold my promise. This commitment drove me to explore every possible avenue for support, from seeking sponsorships and grants to organizing fundraising activities.

This experience was a pivotal moment in my life, teaching me invaluable lessons about leadership, perseverance, and the power of education. It underscored the importance of community, resilience, and the impact one person can have in making a difference. Despite the challenges and the weight of the responsibility, the opportunity to support these young Scholars in their educational journey was a privilege that I cherished deeply. It was a testament to the belief that with determination and collective support, barriers can be overcome, and dreams can be realized.

I first returned to the President's Council and Board of Directors and shared exactly what was happening with them. I leaned on the Council to help pivot our plan to ensure the students could still get what we promised. Jennifer Phillips from WESLI, and a member of the Board of Directors said that they would still take the Scholars through their English program for the first six months virtually and then in-person. That would also give us enough time to raise funds for them to attend Madison College as a virtual student after completing their program at WESLI.

We were not the only ones facing the challenges of the pandemic, so was everyone else. One of the reasons Leading Change Africa made it through the pandemic and continues to thrive today is communication. The lines of communication needed to be open between the families, the schools, the board of directors, and the stakeholders. As a young leader, I learned a lot during this time, and I was thankful to have such supportive individuals surrounding me. I believe that every challenge helps you understand how to move forward in a new way.

I should mention that through all of this, I was not only leading this organization, but I had also started another business called Yam Education. It is an online education platform where individuals can access education 24/7 from anywhere in the world. Yam means Intelligence in the Mossi language in Burkina Faso.

I have always promised myself that I would come to the United States to study and learn the systems here to see how I can go back and improve the situation for my people. Even now, in 2024, in countries like Burkina Faso, education is still lacking because the government hasn't invested in building infrastructure or capacity for teachers.

After coming to the United States and realizing the power of online education, I knew I could leverage this to help more individuals not only access quality education but get the help they need to learn crucial skills so that they're prepared to enter the workforce.

Yam Education partners with Madison College, the University of Wisconsin School systems, and WESLI so that African students can access online courses to gain their Associate Degrees and other certificates without attending crowded schools in Africa. When you're in a classroom with upwards of 2,000 students, it is difficult to really learn the material, let alone build the skills, and leave well-prepared to enter the workforce.

Not only does Yam Education allow one to take courses from leading English institutions, but it also offers teaching assistants, academic advisors, and dedicated tech support to assist students with guidance, assignments, extensions, or navigating the online campus. Additionally, Yam offers group session office hours and free conversation partners for all students studying two or more lessons per week.

Leading Change Africa has been my primary focus, dedicating my efforts and resources to its success without drawing a salary for my work. My commitment to this cause comes from a place of passion and a desire to effect real change rather than financial compensation.

It is not because I don't like money. I think we all need money to be able to survive and to do the things we love. I left a secure, well-paying job to focus on

Leading Change. I took the leap of faith because I believe that if you're willing to work to serve others, you will always be rewarded later on.

The concept of Servant Leadership is very important to me and the way I approach leading my team and Scholars at both YAM and Leading Change Africa.

When I first came to the United States and was interested in pursuing Accounting, I searched the accounting department on the University of Wisconsin-Madison's website. Professor Warfield was the first person to come up, and I reached out to see if I could meet with him to learn more about the program. At the time, I didn't realize he was the chair of accounting.

With an open heart and mind, he invited me into his office, where I laid out my educational plans before him. Professor Warfield graciously outlined a strategic path for me: starting at Madison College to take general courses and save money, then transitioning to the Wisconsin School of Business.

Once I was accepted into the accounting program, Professor Warfield became not just a mentor but a pivotal figure in my education. He introduced me to the concept of servant leadership through a book that profoundly influenced his life.

Recognizing my earlier curiosity about his leadership philosophy, he believed this book could further enrich my understanding and development. His mentorship did not end with my graduation; it evolved into a lasting collaboration, with Professor Warfield joining the Advisory Board for Yam Education. He continues to shape the vision and direction of our work.

Servant leadership is a philosophy that emphasizes serving others first rather than focusing solely on accumulating power or authority. In this approach, the leader's primary goal is to support and enhance the growth, development, and well-being of those they lead. Servant leaders prioritize the needs of their team members, empowering them to reach their full potential and achieve collective goals.

The concept of servant leadership is often attributed to Robert K. Greenleaf, who introduced it in 1970. Greenleaf was an American management expert and organizational theorist who spent much of his career studying leadership and management practices. Greenleaf proposed a radical shift in traditional leadership paradigms, advocating for leaders to adopt a mindset of service and humility. He believed servant leadership could transform organizations and society by fostering trust, collaboration, and mutual respect among individuals.

Greenleaf's ideas gained traction over the years and have influenced numerous leaders across various industries and sectors. Servant leadership has become recognized as a compelling approach to leadership that emphasizes empathy, ethical decision-making, and a commitment to the greater good. It continues to inspire leaders worldwide to prioritize the well-being and development of their followers while striving for positive and meaningful change.

Generational leadership is another leadership approach that I believe is incredibly important and is an attribute of how I've structured Leading Change Africa. You don't have to be the same leader in 10 years as you are today. Generational leadership is an approach that acknowledges and leverages different generations' diverse perspectives, values, and experiences within an organization or society.

This leadership style recognizes that individuals from different generations may have unique strengths, preferences, and communication styles that can contribute to the overall success of an organization and, in this case, an entire country.

Leaders who embrace generational leadership strive to foster collaboration, mutual respect, and cross-generational learning within their teams. They recognize the value of diverse perspectives and seek to create environments where individuals of all generations can thrive and contribute their unique talents.

This is so important because of the challenges we have in Africa as of now. We have leaders who have worked for 20 years and think they are the only ones who can run the country. At some point, it makes the country go backward because they are only thinking about themselves — not the community as a whole.

I argue that Africa is behind because they have not adopted generational or servant leadership. The leaders who come into power only think about themselves and ensure their pocketbooks are full. They place as many family members in leadership positions to ensure they are secure.

The leaders are working to serve themselves rather than thinking about the well-being of their communities.

When you get the privilege to serve others, you really have to serve them.

We need to change the model in Africa. We need to work together to make the next generation different and encourage change.

I often think of Lee Kuan Yew of Singapore. The country was impoverished in the early 1960s when he came into leadership. At this same time, Burkina Faso and other African countries were getting their independence and, therefore, were at a comparable place. In less than 30 years, Singapore changed themselves, and is now on top of the map – financially, industrially, and in every other way — because ONE person decided they wanted to alter the course of the country. That is powerful.

Yew did this by working on three areas: education, tourism, and foreign direct investment. Over 60 years later, Africa is still largely behind and considered one of the poorest countries in the world. It's because there has been leader after leader only thinking about ensuring that their pockets are full and more about power than improving the country.

This has influenced my determination to create change and the mission behind Leading Change Africa: Transforming young Africans into leaders and agents of change.

As you reflect on these insights, it's crucial to ask yourself how you can embody the principles of service-oriented leadership in your own life and community. The need for a new model of leadership in Africa—one that mirrors the selflessness and vision of leaders like Lee Kuan Yew—is clear. Each of us holds the potential to be part of this transformation, whether by mentoring young leaders, investing in community projects, or advocating for policies that prioritize the common good over individual wealth.

Let this chapter serve as a call to action: to commit yourself to serve, to lead with integrity, and to work collectively towards a future where the next generation can inherit a community characterized by prosperity and equity. How will you contribute to changing the leadership model in your community, and what steps will you take to ensure that your service leaves a lasting impact? It begins with the individual choices you make today. I encourage you to be the change you wish to see.

"Human beings are uncut diamonds, but without education, we never fully get to see them shine."

6

Leadership, Education, and Entrepreneurship

You already know I come from Burkina Faso, West Africa. What you may not understand is that Burkina Faso is one of the wealthiest countries in the world and also one of the poorest countries in the world. How can one be rich and poor at the same time?

That's certainly a paradox. But yes, if you are living in a community full of oil and you don't know what oil looks like, you are poor. If you live in a house full of uncut diamonds and don't know what a diamond looks like, you are still poor. You might be thinking about the country's natural resources by this time.

The country has natural resources, but I am referring to its people. I genuinely believe that human beings are uncut diamonds. But because of a lack of education, we never fully get to see them shine. That is one of the reasons why I have always wanted to leave, go to America, get an excellent education, and return to help my own people.

Our mission at Leading Change is to transform young Africans into leaders and leaders into agents of change. To transform 1,024 African youth and leaders by 2030 and positively influence 1 million individuals by 2050.

Our model is different from most programs.

Leading Change strives to lay the foundation for future change by providing access to high-quality education, leadership development, mentorship guidance, community service opportunities, real-world job experience, and driving entrepreneurial pursuits.

We believe that when one is empowered with knowledge, it is their duty to change other people's lives.

This is why, following graduation, all LCA Scholars are required to:

- Work for another company in the US or Africa

for three years
- Sponsor another student of Leading Change to pay it forward
- Start their own business in Africa to ignite change and create more jobs, after three years working in the US or Africa.

We partner with high schools in Nigeria, Mali, Malawi, Rwanda, and Burkina Faso, Africa. While we initially began working with young Africans in Burkina Faso, we wanted to expand and give more kids a chance at this opportunity. We receive the top 20 applications from each school and then narrow down the applicants. When writing this book in 2024, we had approximately 500 applicants applying, and we only could serve 125 each year. As the organization grows, so will our capacity to serve.

Scholars can begin applying for the program in 10th Grade. To be considered for the program, they must submit an application highlighting their academic performance, skills, and aspirations. As part of the application process, students write three essays, send letters of recommendation, and commit to attending our six-month leadership program after being admitted.

The leadership program is the most critical part of our organization. The transformation starts from day one. After being pre-selected as a Leading Change Scholar, students are expected to attend a six-month Discovery Program. This program is the first transition step in assisting students with the admission process to college in the United States, Burkina Faso, Rwanda, and Mauritius, Africa.

The mission's fundamental purpose is to lay the foundation for future change. The organization aims to ignite people's spirits, touch their hearts, and transform their lives.

Colleges and universities are platforms of education that assist in the process of achieving these objectives. However, they are not the only means by which we measure the success of our mission. Our Scholars are sculpted into leaders by focusing on community service, leadership training, and entrepreneurial pursuits. At Leading Change, we are motivated and driven by three significant expectations for ourselves:

- Transforming young Africans to discover the "big picture" in the small details; by building the foundation of the future today, we can reach a higher tomorrow.

- Asking our Scholars to challenge themselves to become trusted citizens, crucial contributors, valued members of society, and impactful leaders.
- Growing our Scholars and exposing them to new visions and perspectives to break the barriers of the past.

At Leading Change Africa, we have designed four core program areas to provide comprehensive support and guidance to our Scholars as they begin their journey toward becoming successful leaders and agents of change. We accept applications for our programs four times a year to ensure they align with our partner programs and schools.

At the heart of our mission lies the Leadership Academy. This program is a platform where young minds are encouraged to step beyond their comfort zones, embracing challenges that refine their character and enhance their capacity for leadership. Here, Scholars are not only students but visionaries in training, poised to embrace roles as trusted citizens and pivotal contributors within their communities and the broader society.

The Leadership Academy's importance is to instill rich perspectives and guiding values within our Scholars. It's a nurturing ground for personal growth, where the ideals of diversity, empathy, and integrity are taught and lived. This environment cultivates a sense of responsibility and a drive to effect positive change, laying the groundwork for Scholars to emerge as leaders who inspire and encourage change.

Much of our program focuses on community service and paying it forward. Unlike in many parts of the world, the concept of giving back through student organizations or community initiatives is still a relatively non-existent concept across Africa. In recognizing this gap, we encourage our Scholars to become change agents—motivating them to establish and lead clubs, participate in a presidents' council, and actively contribute to their communities. This engagement goes beyond enhancing their academic portfolio; it's about crafting a legacy of service and leadership that distinguishes them as competitive, holistic candidates for scholarships and future opportunities.

Building on the foundation laid by the Leadership Academy, our College Preparatory program represents the next critical phase in our Scholars' journey. This program is designed to help navigate the complex college admissions process, providing Scholars with the comprehensive support necessary to unlock doors to prestigious higher education institutions worldwide.

The transition from the Leadership Academy to the College Preparatory program is a seamless continuation of our commitment to holistic development. Recognizing the pivotal role of technology in modern education and entrepreneurship, we place a special emphasis on computer literacy—a skill I personally know the value of all too well. Having not owned a computer until the age of 18 and only being introduced to the concept of computers and the internet in high school, I understand the challenges faced by many of our Scholars. In a world where technological proficiency is often taken for granted, the reality in many parts of Africa is starkly different. The ability to navigate digital spaces, from typing to researching, was crucial to my academic success and has become indispensable in my entrepreneurial endeavors.

Therefore, as part of the College Preparatory program, we ensure our Scholars are not just academically prepared but technologically proficient. Through personalized mentorship, we introduce them to the essentials of computer usage, from basic typing skills to more advanced digital literacy, ensuring they are on equal footing with their global counterparts. Many of our Scholars have not owned or used a computer before. Coupled with academic enrichment, standardized testing preparation, and assistance with crafting compelling application essays, our program aims to equip Scholars with a well-rounded skill set.

Moreover, we emphasize mastering English and understanding its critical role in accessing global educational resources and opportunities. This dual focus on language and technology prepares our Scholars not only to gain admission but also to excel within the competitive environment of higher education.

As our Scholars transition into higher education, the Post-Secondary Education program stands ready to support their continued growth academically and professionally. This program encompasses personalized mentoring, valuable internship placements, and expansive professional networking opportunities. These components are designed to ensure our Scholars can excel in their fields and forge impactful careers.

Integral to this phase of development is our commitment to cultivating the next generation of leaders, entrepreneurs, and agents of change. Through regular weekly meetings, we engage our Scholars in deep discussions, skill-building sessions, and leadership exercises that challenge them to think critically and act decisively. This hands-on approach to leadership and entrepreneurial education highlights our core belief: true success surpasses the boundaries of academic achievements; it shapes individuals who are equipped with a diverse set of skills, grounded in ethical values, and driven by a clear vision for the future.

We envision our Scholars not merely as graduates with degrees but as visionary leaders ready to undertake transformative roles in society. By instilling in them the principles of servant leadership and providing them with the tools to navigate the complexities of the modern world, we are preparing them to effect positive change, inspire innovation, and lead with compassion and integrity.

Building on the foundational knowledge and skills developed in the Post-Secondary Education program, our Accelerators program is designed to lead Scholars through the intricacies of launching and nurturing their startups. Through dedicated mentorship, advanced technology training, and crucial funding access, we equip aspiring entrepreneurs with the resources to transform their innovative ideas into sustainable businesses.

The Accelerators program is structured around two intensive cohorts, focusing on the idea generation and validation phases. Within these cohorts, Scholars are immersed in an environment of rigorous feedback and support from mentors and industry experts, ensuring their entrepreneurial visions are both viable and impactful. This process pushes Scholars to think creatively and act boldly.

Central to our approach is cultivating a culture of innovation and creativity. We encourage our Scholars to devise solutions that address the challenges facing their communities and the world at large. The program aims to mold our Scholars into visionary leaders and changemakers ready to make their mark in changing the future of Africa.

Reflecting on my personal journey, the integration of alternative spring breaks into our Accelerators program is deeply intentional. Inspired by my experiences of community service during college—journeys that took me from Tampa to New York and beyond—these breaks are designed to broaden our Scholars' horizons. Participating in projects like those at the Grand Canyon, our Scholars not only contribute to vital environmental conservation efforts but also forge meaningful connections with diverse communities. These initiatives highlight the essence of impactful leadership: the ability to translate vision into action, underscored by a commitment to service and community engagement.

Each of our programs is designed to inspire young Africans to embrace their passions and pursue their dreams—and from that, a ripple effect will occur. Through motivation, dedication, and follow-through, their visions can be realized. They will impact their families, communities, countries, and the world through their personal fulfillment, contribution to society, and service to others.

In addition to our core programs, I feel it's necessary to share the values of Leading Change Africa. Values are the guiding principles in our lives, and leadership occurs within the context of our core values.

Understanding and embracing our core values stands at the foundation of everything we do. They are practical guiding principles that shape our leadership and personal development approach. In our view, leadership unfolds within the framework of these deeply held beliefs.

Our values are an invitation to live and lead with integrity, to kindle respect in diversity, and to embody authenticity in every action. They are not static but dynamically engaged through our leadership practices and programs.

- **Integrity** manifests as the backbone of trust, urging our Scholars to stand firm in their ethical convictions and honor their commitments.
- **Respect** ensures we cherish the dignity of every individual, embracing our differences with empathy and compassion.
- **Authenticity** encourages a harmony between beliefs and actions, fostering a life of purpose and positive influence on others.
- **Courage** calls us to advocate for the common good, even in the face of adversity, championing inclusion and justice.
- **Service** emphasizes a commitment that stretches beyond individual gains, dedicated to a cause greater than oneself.
- **Humility** invites a reflective stance on our limitations, welcoming diverse perspectives with grace.
- **Wisdom** guides our decision-making with a balanced view of human dynamics, considering the long-term impact on all stakeholders.
- **Making a Difference** encapsulates our ultimate

goal: to leave an indelible mark that positively transforms lives, systems, and organizations.

Each of these values weaves through the fabric of Leading Change Africa, shaping our Scholars into leaders who aspire to achieve and inspire. As we guide our Scholars to align their actions with these core values, we unlock the potential for transformative impact, far surpassing the outcomes of traditional leadership development.

Through this values-centered approach, we cultivate leaders equipped to navigate the complexities of our world with wisdom, empathy, and a relentless drive to effect meaningful change.

Failure, Fear, and Success

"Failure and success are mirror images." – *Steve Johnson*

For us to achieve the level of success that we desire, we need to overcome obstacles and understand that every failure opens a new opportunity.

Abraham Lincoln was born into poverty and faced defeat throughout his life. He lost eight elections, failed twice in business, and suffered a nervous breakdown, only to become one of the greatest presidents in the U.S.

Among the world's greatest inventors and scientists, Thomas Edison failed innumerable times before he was finally driven to discover the genius that slept within his brain.

Helen Keller became deaf, mute, and blind. Despite her great misfortune, she has written her name indelibly in history. Her entire life served as evidence that no one ever is defeated until defeat has been accepted as a reality.

Hillary Clinton failed the D.C. bar exam, only to pass the one in Arkansas and eventually become one of the most politically influential women in the United States.

Beethoven was deaf, and Milton was blind, but their names will last as long as time endures because they dreamed and translated their dreams into organized thought and action.

The list is not exhaustive. Obstacles exist to signify how badly we want to move forward. Failure is a passageway to success; how we respond to failure will ultimately determine our success.

So, what does success mean? For me, success means a warm home, a trip abroad, a healthy relationship, a family life, a birthday present, and a college education for my children. Success means winning admiration, earning leadership status, and being looked up to by family, friends, and business associates. Success means self-respect and continuous personal growth. Success means freedom: freedom from fear, doubt, worry, frustration, anxiety, and financial problems. Success means achievement, a goal reached, and a dream come true.

By my definition of success, you might agree with me that we all want to succeed. We were born with the seed of greatness within us and deserve to enjoy all the good things in life. There is no question about it. But we must first believe that success is possible and dreams are permitted.

When you believe your dreams are possible, you'll likely take daily actions to ensure you get what you desire and accomplish your goals. You'll also likely do what it takes to overcome the obstacles standing in your way, even in the face of challenges.

However, in many countries, like Burkina Faso,

Africa, the opportunity is missing, and dreams never really feel entirely within reach, leaving most of the population to continue being held back by the barriers that have existed for generations.

When dreams never really feel in reach, it's hard to be motivated or determined to strive for better. Leading Change Africa is here to give them a chance to dream.

Rasmata's future was to become a housewife. And that was it.

"I was a girl with an outdated belief. For a girl in my country, it's a belief that you don't need to study that much at school. You just need to get the basics and, later on, get married, and that's it. But with Leading Change, I learned that I CAN speak up for myself, I CAN have goals, and I CAN do better than just being a housewife.

Leading change has been updating the person I am.

We are learning how to do public speaking, how to manage our time, and how to develop ourselves. We want to make a change, and they want to create leaders who are ready to change communities. I'm really grateful for that."

It's not just a girl or her immediate family who benefits from quality education; it's her entire country.

Studies have shown that when 10% more of the girls in a given country attend school, the country's gross domestic product increases by an average of 3%, which can make a huge difference in a developing economy.

And Grace, he never thought he would be speaking English or have a chance at achieving his dream of working with electronics. Now, it's a part of his daily life.

*"Leading Change changed my point of view in the world. I now have an entrepreneurial mindset: **never give up, always give it your best**. It impacted my life and my entire personality.*

I am working on starting my business now. I am creating a simple sensor that people can put in their houses so that if the lights are left on, the electronic device will turn them off. It will help the entire country because there is not enough electricity for everyone.

When I was back in high school, I didn't know much about entrepreneurship; I was trying to get good grades and strive for a secure job. When I learned about the mission of Leading Change Africa, I no longer wanted just to graduate and find a secure job. I wanted to participate in the success of my country.

The six-month training helped me develop my English skills. I never figured I would speak English like I am right now. It's amazing. It also allowed me to become comfortable with public speaking. I learned how to develop and share my ideas and create a business plan.

If there's one thing I want to say, it's thank you. Thank you for the leadership, for being here, for supporting Africans like us, and for trying to do the best for ourselves to impact our communities. Thank you." — Grace

These stories reveal that success is more than personal achievements; it's about overcoming barriers, personal growth, and the ability to dream big. Their experiences showcase that individuals can surpass societal expectations and contribute significantly to their communities with belief, education, and support.

Now, before I move on, I'd like to share another personal story about failure — and that admitting defeat can be the first step toward success.

Beyond the Shadows of Fear: Learning from Miriam and Salimata

In college, I dated a beautiful woman, Miriam, who has become a very successful businesswoman, wife, and mother. Miriam was outgoing, always happy, and loved life with a passion. Her energy and outgoing personality drew me to her the most. She was never afraid to try something new or accept a challenge.

Miriam's best friend, Salimata, who hung out with us often, was the complete opposite. She was introverted, worried about everything, and always feared something would go wrong. In fact, she was so different that I often wondered how they could actually enjoy each other's company.

As time went on, Miriam graduated college and landed a successful career. She and Salimata went their separate ways as their lifestyles no longer connected, and their outlook on life had changed— it was nothing bad; it just didn't fit anymore. It happens to all of us.

Unlike Miriam, Salimata struggled to hold down a job. People always gave her opportunities, but she couldn't make anything work. It wasn't that she didn't try—she definitely did—but something else held her back.

One day, Salimata decided to reach out to Miriam and asked if she'd be willing to meet and reconnect with her. Miriam agreed, and a couple of weeks later, they met in Miriam's office. Greeting each other with open arms and big hugs, they exchanged small talk and reminisced about the good times in college.

Then there was a silence in the room — Salimata let down her guard and said, *"I came to see you because I have fallen on desperate times. It doesn't matter what I do; I just can't seem to make my life work. I get a job, and it is fine at first, but then I end up hating it and eventually leave. I keep on trying to make things work, but the more I try, the worse things seem to get. I wanted to ask you what your secret is. why are you so successful?"*

Miriam sat quietly for a moment, with so many thoughts swirling around in her head.

Then she shared, *"There is no secret — my success lies in the mindset I use to approach life. I have learned to have a great attitude about life, to see the glass as half-full instead of half-empty, and whenever I am about to do something, I ask myself if what I am about to do is motivated by love or fear. For example, before I go into an important business meeting, I ask myself if what I am about to say is motivated by my passion for the meeting's purpose or is it motivated by a fear that my ideas might be rejected or something might go wrong."*

What Miriam shared with Salimata was so powerful. Most people are motivated to take action because they fear the consequences if they don't. This is silly when you think about it. People make up a fear and then act based on a fear that doesn't exist. They create a fear and then set themselves up to protect it.

All this does is take them further away from their ultimate goal. Always remember what you focus on, you will find. Focus on the fear, and that is what you get. Focus on what you want, and that is what you get. When your motivations are intentional and based on love, you will naturally draw to you what you want.

Fear is one of the greatest challenges we face today, as individuals and as a society. Fear holds us back from the fullest expression of ourselves; it prevents us from loving ourselves and others.

Often, we fear rejection, so we avoid asking for the things we really need. Or we refuse to commit ourselves because of the risk of failure. It is important to distinguish between fears that help us and those that hurt us. Because of our fears, many of us compromise and settle for less.

Much of our fear stems from an incomplete sense of identity. We may fear disapproval or rejection by others because we tend to see our self-worth as being dependent on their good opinion. But once we know our talents and our purpose, we will never again experience that particular fear.

Perhaps you've heard the old saying, *"What you don't know won't hurt you."* Nothing could be further from the truth. Ignorance is never bliss. Instead, it produces fear and confusion. However, once you know the multitude of your blessings and how you can help others, the shadow of false fear will no longer have power over you.

I often explain FEAR as *false evidence that appears real*, and any action motivated by love is always best.

As I mentioned at the beginning of this chapter, Burkina Faso is one of the richest and also one of the poorest countries in the world. That may seem like an odd pairing of words: "rich" and "poor" side by side. We will attempt to overturn this paradox in our lifetime. But now, I want to reflect on another paradox: celebrating failure.

Celebrating failure is another paradox, but it is one of the most important paradoxical phrases worth learning and remembering. What makes me believe so? Because

It may seem that Salimata failed, but it is not actually the case.

The more I talked with Mariam, the more I realized that Salimata's case was hopeful. Mariam strongly believes that fear of failure is the number one killer of grand plans and good ideas. More than a lack of knowledge or skill or a clear strategy or action plan, the biggest obstacle in the way of progress for individuals is the paralysis caused by the fear of failing.

Most of us learn early in life that failure is bad, even shameful. We learn to hide our failures, make excuses for them, or ignore them. Worse yet, when we stop taking risks, we become more cautious in avoiding the possibility of failing. We start limiting our choices to only those actions with a high probability of success.

And so, our choices become limited, and our field of play becomes smaller. But, it does not have to be that way.

Instead, we should embrace failure and see it as one of the most important ways to learn and move forward. As one of my favorite authors would say, *"One way to learn how to do something right is to do it wrong — but don't stay there too long!"*

Failing at any action, even failing to take action, is a rich learning opportunity. It is an opportunity that is worth exploring, reflecting on, and celebrating.

If you feel bound by fear and afraid of taking actions that could potentially enrich your life, I encourage you to reflect on the words of J.K. Rowling: *"It's impossible to live without failing at something unless you lived so cautiously that you might as well not lived at all, in which case you failed by default."*

Reflect on what success truly means to you. Is it a solitary journey to the top, or is it the paths you pave for others to follow? In the stories within these pages, we've witnessed resilience and hope that underscore the fact that success is intricately woven with the lives we influence and the dreams we inspire.

Each of us possesses a unique power—the power to illuminate paths, to lift others from the shadows of uncertainty and fear, and to believe in the potential that resides in the hearts of those around us.

How will you use this power? Will you extend your hand in mentorship, lending your voice to those who've yet to find theirs? Will you stand in advocacy for dreams that have been silenced by circumstance? Or will you simply believe in someone, offering the kind of support that can turn their life around?

Your actions, no matter how big or small they seem, are the ripples that can create massive change, transforming not just individual lives but entire communities.

"Goals allow us to decide what our lives look like from here on out."

7

Beyond Dreams: The Power of Goal Setting

Realizing your dreams includes setting goals and having a plan to achieve them. A goal is a dream being acted upon. It's an objective, a purpose, and a promise of the future. Goals allow us to decide what our lives look like from here on out. What you were yesterday, you paid for. What you are today, tomorrow, next month, or the rest of your life, you get to decide.

However, a goal will only be a dream if action is not taken to reach it. Now is the time to start working on your dreams so that the next five years will look very different from where you are today. Now is the time to prepare for the future so that you don't meet it with apprehension but with anticipation.

If you don't make plans for your future, you'll likely fall into someone else's plan — a plan that doesn't match your goals or dreams. One that has you going through the motions rather than living your purpose.

"We all need lots of powerful long-range goals to help us past the short-term obstacles," Jim Rohn said.

As I mentioned before, success typically doesn't come without some type of failure first. How you choose to face the failure and the obstacles makes all the difference.

For leaders, setting clear and ambitious goals is a roadmap for guiding teams toward a shared mission and vision. Beyond direction, goals foster a sense of motivation and engagement among team members, igniting a collective drive to strive for excellence and surpass expectations.

Moreover, goal setting promotes focus and prioritization, enabling organizations to allocate resources efficiently and tackle high-priority initiatives first. By measuring progress against established goals, leaders can hold themselves and their teams accountable, building a culture of accountability and ownership.

This culture nurtures a spirit of innovation and creativity as individuals are encouraged to explore new approaches and embrace change. Through goal setting, organizations cultivate resilience, adaptability, and a commitment to continuous improvement, laying the foundation for sustainable success.

Within our programs, Scholars are challenged to set both long-term and short-term objectives. Long-term goals represent the future we envision for ourselves and our communities. These goals, spanning three, five, and ten years into the future, are bold and audacious, designed to inspire and motivate us to overcome obstacles and pursue our passions relentlessly.

In contrast, short-term goals are stepping stones towards our long-term aspirations, providing actionable targets for immediate focus and progress. These goals, spanning days, weeks, and months, are tangible and achievable, serving as confidence builders as we navigate the journey toward our larger dreams. By setting and achieving short-term goals, Scholars develop momentum and resilience, empowering them to navigate the complexities of their educational, professional, and personal journey and emerge as leaders poised to effect positive change in their communities and beyond.

Here are a few examples of resilient young leaders whose journey from Burkina Faso to quality education and entrepreneurship is a testament to the impact of education, mentorship, and opportunity.

From Ouagadougou to Global Change Maker

Wilfried was born and raised in Ouagadougou, Burkina Faso. He comes from a family of five. In 9th grade, Wilfried dreamed of studying abroad when he learned about Leading Change Africa. The following year, Wilfried worked hard, applied, and was accepted into the Leading Change program. It was a dream come true.

In 2019, he came to the United States to study English at WESLI and to earn a TESL certificate. He would return to Burkina Faso to teach English and leadership courses to other young Africans at the Leading Change Center.

In 2021, Wilfried returned to the United States to attend college. I'm proud to say that he graduated from Madison College with an Associate degree in science-pre-engineering and plans to continue his education and major in Computer Engineering.

Wilfried shares, "Leading Change has helped me pursue higher education in the US and improve my English and leadership skills, which has broadened my view about the world. It has allowed me to think about my career goals and ways to use my knowledge and skills to contribute to the development of Africa.

Having the opportunity to teach back in Burkina and working closely with the administration office at the leading change center helped me build patience, balance in my life, and resilience, which was important during difficult times."

Wilfried now envisions his future with hope. He aspires to be someone whose work contributes to making the world a better place.

How Hawa Turned Barriers Into Stepping Stones

When Hawa was in 7th grade, she told one of her oldest brothers that she wanted to go to the United States to continue her studies.

Her brother asked her, "How are you going to get there? You don't have money. There are no scholarships to go to the United States."

Determined and hopeful, Hawa's response was, "I'll do all I can, and whatever will happen, I know I will have done my best."

As the years passed, Hawa continued to work hard in school, and tenth grade, she learned about Leading Change Africa. It was at that time she knew her dream WAS possible.

In 12th grade, she was finally able to apply for the scholarship. The application consisted of submitting her report cards and three essays sharing more about who she was, her beliefs, and her values, and most importantly, the reason she should be selected for the program.

As I'm sure you guessed by now, Hawa was accepted into the program. She began an intensive six-month training program with Leading Change in Burkina Faso, where she learned and studied the English language, leadership, and business skills.

After completing the six-month program, she applied again to be selected to come to the United States to attend Madison College in Wisconsin. The application process serves as a model of real-world challenges, emphasizing the values of hard work, critical thinking, and determination necessary to achieve one's goals in life. This application aimed to demonstrate proficiency in the English language, a vital skill for success in academia and beyond. Additionally, applicants were required to showcase their understanding of fundamental principles of leadership and teamwork, underscoring the importance of these qualities in navigating life and their path toward a successful future.

Since she was a little girl, Hawa had dreamed of coming to the United States. When she found out she had been accepted into the program again and had the opportunity to study there, her dream came true.

"I am the sixth of eight siblings." She shared that even

though her brothers and sisters did well in school and were the first in their program, they had to put their studies at a university on hold because they didn't have the financial resources to continue.

Hawa said, "I was afraid of having the same fate, but Leading Change has given me the chance to continue, and I am beyond thankful for that."

Hawa's goals for the future include:

- Attending a top University to pursue her career in computer engineering
- Becoming a professor so she can share her knowledge and passion with others
- Starting her own tech company in Burkina Faso, Africa, to give others a chance to live their dreams — just like she has.

Hawa's dreams are possible thanks to the generous individuals supporting Leading Change Africa — as leaders, donors, and mentors.

Bridging the Gap in Agriculture

"I wonder how things would've turned out if I hadn't had this opportunity with Leading Change Africa? Where would I be now?"

As a young child, Kendrixe was told to do well in school, especially in English and Math, so that she could continue her studies in an English-speaking country. She never fully understood why but always tried her best.

Kendrixe's mom was a school teacher and taught in rural areas in Burkina Faso, so Kendrixe and her siblings lived with their Dad in the city. Their mother would visit on the weekends, but their father mainly supported her and her three siblings.

In high school, Kendrixe became the President of the English Club, and that was where she learned about Leading Change.

She shared, "We had learned English in school, and we knew everything 'on paper,' but we never learned how to speak it. And Leading Change wanted to teach us how! I learned all about their program and knew I had to be a part of it. When my Senior year approached, I could finally apply and was accepted!"

Fast forward, Kendrixe's twin sister, Ashley, both completed the leadership program and were selected to come to the United States. When writing this book, Kendrixe had graduated from Madison Technical College and is now attending the University of Wisconsin-Madison, majoring in Electrical Engineering.

Kendrixe's long-term goal for the future is to participate in the development of Burkina Faso, focusing on agricultural development.

Kendrixe said, *"We have the resources and the people willing to work, but we lack the necessary knowledge and technology to implement. More than 80% of the population are farmers or a part of an Agricultural area, yet we cannot feed everyone adequately.*

We still use archaic tools for farming. My goal is to make farming technology and machines available to our communities. With these machines, we can utilize the people currently working in the fields to work in other areas that would benefit the country and its advancement. It would be life-changing for so many people in Africa.

I am grateful for Leading Change's support of my studies. I feel empowered and know that I have peo-

ple supporting my dreams and keeping me on track, ensuring my eyes are always on the goal!"

Through the lens of their stories, we witness first-hand the profound impact of setting both long-term and short-term goals. Long-term goals represent the culmination of dreams, inspiring perseverance and resilience in the face of adversity. They propel Scholars forward, igniting a passion for progress and a commitment to realizing their full potential.

Conversely, short-term goals offer tangible milestones on the path to long-term success, providing Scholars with immediate targets for focus and progress. These achievable objectives serve as building blocks for confidence, empowering Scholars to navigate the complexities of their journey with purpose and determination. By setting and achieving short-term goals, Scholars cultivate a sense of agency and momentum, laying the groundwork for sustained growth and achievement.

As we celebrate the accomplishments of Wilfried, Hawa, Kendrixe, and countless other resilient young leaders, we are reminded of the power of education, mentorship, and opportunity to shape the future of Africa. It's essential to reflect on how goal setting shapes not only the individual trajectories of

Scholars but also the broader landscape of their communities and the continent as a whole.

These narratives encourage you to examine the role of goal setting in your life. Think about how setting focused and intentional goals can transform your own journey and positively impact those around you. Let the successes of these young leaders inspire you to embrace goal setting as a vital tool for personal achievement and as a means to contribute to the broader progress of your business and community. Your commitment to your goals as a leader can serve as a model for others, showing the way to personal fulfillment and collective advancement.

"It is smarter to start with what we really want, ...and then work backward to figure out what we need to do..."

8

Fueling Change with Resilience

Entrepreneurship isn't for everyone. It's for those bold enough to chase their passions and carve their paths in the world. It's for the movers, the shakers, and the relentless go-getters who refuse to settle for anything less than extraordinary.

Entrepreneurship isn't your average 9-5 job. It's a calling, a passion, and a way of life. It's about rolling up your sleeves, taking risks, and making things happen against all odds.

I'm talking about all the late nights fueled by determination and too much caffeine, the moments of doubt when you wonder if you're crazy for chasing your dreams, or the times when you look at your bank account and are not sure where your next paycheck is coming from.

Above all, entrepreneurship is about knowing WHY you do what you do and letting that drive you forward, even when things get tough. For me, entrepreneurship is personal. It's about honoring my roots, my upbringing, and the journey that brought me here — leading to my own for-profit and not-for-profit organizations so that I can change the future for millions of people in Africa. As you've read throughout the pages, it's about turning challenges into opportunities and paving the way for others to follow in my footsteps.

At the end of the day, it's not about the fancy titles or the size of your bank account. It's about the lives you touch, the communities you uplift, and the legacy you leave behind.

As you know, I left my full-time job to pursue Leading Change Africa and Yam Education full-time. What I didn't tell you is that a major financial firm proposed to hire me and offered me more money than I ever dreamed of. I have to admit that the offer was tempting, but I had my values clear and already thought of this eventuality. I thanked them for thinking of me and kindly turned down the offer.

This is what the firm failed to understand: while making money is good, it is not my primary motivation. I believe that having meaningful work and meaningful relationships is far better. To me, meaningful work is being on a mission I become engrossed in, and meaningful relationships are those I have with people I care deeply about and who care deeply about me.

Think about it: it's senseless to have making money as your goal, as money has no intrinsic value. The value of money comes from what it can buy, and it certainly can't buy everything. Some of the best times that I have valued didn't cost me anything.

It is smarter to start with what we really want, which are our real goals and what matters most to us, and then work backward to figure out what we need to do to attain them. Let's make it clear: money is important. It is as important as the food it buys and the necessities of life that we can afford. But money is not the only thing we need and certainly not the most important one once we get past having the amount we need to be comfortable.

When thinking about what we really want, it pays to think of their relative values so we weigh them properly. In my case, I wanted meaningful work and meaningful relationships equally, and I value money less as long as I have enough to take care of my basic needs.

As you continue to read the stories of Scholars and individuals who have overcome all the odds, I challenge you to embrace your entrepreneurial spirit with open arms. Lean into your passions, harness your strengths, and don't be afraid to blaze your own trail.

Because the truth is, the world is waiting for your unique offering, so it's up to you to not only dream big but to take action.

From Electrical Sales to Championing Women in Tech

Frida's entrepreneurial journey is one of resilience, determination, and a commitment to breaking down cultural barriers in her community in Cameroon. Born and raised in the English-speaking region of Cameroon, Frida's story is symbolic of the struggles faced by many young women striving for independence and empowerment in a society where traditional gender roles often prevail.

Growing up, Frida observed a stark divide between

the opportunities available to men and women in her community. Women were typically expected to fulfill domestic roles, with aspirations for education and entrepreneurship often discouraged.

Frida went on to excel in school and obtained a degree in banking and finance. One of her first jobs was working with an electrical company selling transformers and electrical poles in Cameroon. Determined to make some extra money, Frida started her own business selling electrical cables. The company she was working for had sold everything but the cables. She saw cables as necessary for a company buying poles and transformers.

As Frida started her business, she quickly realized that people needed more than just the cables; they needed the knowledge behind how these cables worked. But without an electrical engineering background, Frida couldn't answer their questions, leading to frustration on both sides of sales. Frida ended up partnering with an individual knowledgeable in that area so they could help with the technical end, and she could focus on sales. Unfortunately, she learned of their dishonesty shortly after bringing on this partner, and the company quickly failed.

Frida remained undeterred despite facing these

setbacks and challenges. While trying to navigate her path and deciding where to go next, she recognized the lack of support and mentorship for young women entrepreneurs in her community. She knew she wanted to focus on empowering others.

She began collaborating with other senior entrepreneurs who were passionate about encouraging young people to become self-employed instead of waiting for the government to respond as the unemployment rate continued to increase.

After offering these services for some time, Frida recognized a significant gender gap in entrepreneurship, with fewer women showing interest than men. This realization ignited her passion even more for empowering young women entrepreneurs and led her to establish the African Enterprising Woman initiative. Through this initiative, Frida aims to provide training, mentorship, and support to women, equipping them with the skills and confidence needed to build sustainable businesses.

Throughout all of this, Frida was introduced to Leading Change Africa, which she says has enabled her to gain essential leadership skills and insights. Participating in the accelerator program, Frida immersed herself in learning and collaboration, embracing the practical resources and interactive platform Leading Change offers.

The program not only equipped Frida with valuable business knowledge but also provided her with a supportive community of like-minded individuals. Through Leading Change, she was able to formalize her business, establish a team, and broaden her impact on women's entrepreneurship in Cameroon.

Frida's work extends beyond traditional entrepreneurship. She also founded Girl Tech, a startup focused on training female software developers and UI/UX designers. By addressing the gender gap in the tech industry, Frida continues to champion inclusivity and diversity, paving the way for future generations of women in technology.

Despite facing cultural and societal barriers, Frida remains steadfast in her commitment to empowering women and fostering economic independence. Her journey is one of hope and inspiration, demonstrating the power of education, mentorship, and resilience in overcoming adversity.

As Frida continues to break down barriers and create opportunities for women in Cameroon, her story stands as a testament to the limitless potential of female entrepreneurs in shaping a more inclusive and equitable society.

How One Program Ignited a Healthcare Evolution

Much like Frida's, Idris' journey is a powerful testament to the transformative potential of the Accelerator Program at Leading Change Africa. Now, as the CEO of The Blue-Pink Center for Women's Health and diligently practicing medicine in Nigeria, Idris embodies the realization of a vision brought to life through determination, support, and the right opportunities.

The Accelerator Program offered Idris skills and knowledge essential for entrepreneurship and a sense of community that continues to be a place he can look to for guidance and inspiration.

A highlight of the Accelerator experience is the business competition that the Scholars take part in. The competition is similar to today's reality television show, *Shark Tank*, where Scholars pitch their business ideas to secure funding so that they can move their vision forward. For many, like Idris, it's their first time preparing and presenting before an audience and judges. This crucial moment tests their abilities and equips them with invaluable experience in articulation and persuasion, vital skills for any aspiring entrepreneur.

Winning this competition marks one of Idris's most significant achievements. It has allowed him to advance his mission to address an issue deeply personal to him—the establishment of a comprehensive Cancer Program in Nigeria. Motivated by the loss of a close family friend to cancer—a loss heightened by inadequate medical resources—Idris is driven to ensure better healthcare access and education in his home country. His vision extends beyond immediate care, aiming to influence governmental policies and foster sustainable health solutions.

Idris's commitment to making a difference doesn't stop with his professional endeavors. He actively mentors young business owners and students, guiding them with the insights and learnings from his journey. This mentorship reflects the core of Leading Change Africa's Program impact: equipping Scholars with the confidence and competence to inspire and lead others to become change agents.

Idris expresses gratitude to the donors and staff at Leading Change. "It's through their generosity that Scholars like me, from a world many may never visit, can have life-changing opportunities that cause a ripple effect far beyond the individual—it's transformative for entire communities."

As you've learned by now, at Leading Change Africa, part of our mission is to empower young Scholars to realize their entrepreneurial visions and drive meaningful change in their communities. One of our programs, the twelve-week Accelerator, is designed to provide Scholars with the tools, resources, and mentorship needed to turn their ideas into successful ventures. Throughout the program, participants are guided through the process of creating a comprehensive business plan, refining their strategies, and setting actionable goals to bring their vision to life.

What sets our Accelerator program apart is its emphasis on real-world experience and practical skill development. Scholars are encouraged to dream big, roll up their sleeves, and immerse themselves in the field. Through hands-on workshops, mentorship sessions, and networking opportunities, participants gain invaluable insights into the intricacies of running a business, navigating challenges, and seizing opportunities in the market.

In addition, after graduating from our program, Scholars in the United States must pursue job opportunities in the US and stay there for at least three years before returning to Africa to focus on their own companies. This requirement may seem counter intuitive to some, but it serves a crucial purpose.

Working in a professional setting provides Scholars invaluable exposure to industry dynamics, market trends, and best practices. By immersing themselves in a corporate environment, Scholars gain firsthand experience in areas such as project management, financial analysis, marketing strategies, leadership, and customer relations—all of which are essential skills for successful entrepreneurship.

Moreover, working in the US exposes Scholars to diverse perspectives, cultures, and business models. This exposure fosters creativity, adaptability, and a global mindset—invaluable qualities in today's interconnected world. By learning from different industries and engaging with diverse teams, Scholars broaden their horizons and cultivate the cross-cultural competencies needed to thrive in the global marketplace. Scholars can access a vast network of professionals, mentors, and potential collaborators.

At the heart of the stories you read throughout this book lies a compelling 'why' — a personal mission that fuels their drive and determination to innovate and change. These resilient young leaders remind us that true leadership and entrepreneurship are grounded in purpose over profit. What is your 'why'? How does it motivate you to keep going, even through the challenging times?

"...it only takes 3% of people to achieve monumental shifts..."

9

Transforming Tomorrow

As I reflect on my journey from my childhood in the vibrant landscapes of Africa to becoming an entrepreneur in the United States, there is one constant — my heart is rooted in the soil of Burkina Faso, and I am passionate about creating a better, more innovative future for my people. My homeland, with its rich heritage and resilient spirit, faces a complex array of challenges and opportunities. The leadership and government structure, often caught in the ebb and flow of political instability, shape the dynamics of both power and progress.

Burkina Faso has experienced a tumultuous political history marked by periods of instability, terrorism, and transitions between different forms of governance. This has shaped the way power is exercised and perceived within the country. Leadership often revolves around a central figure or party, and this concentration of power can impact everything from policy-making to the allocation of resources. The government's ability to implement reforms and foster a conducive environment for growth is crucial. However, governance issues, corruption, and political unrest have historically hindered our progress.

Often, leaders are elected and stay in the position for many years without creating change or advancing the country for the good of the people and future generations. They're solely focused on filling their pockets and ensuring that only their families are set up for success. When power is concentrated in the hands of a few, it limits access to opportunities for the broader population, hindering everything from education to job opportunities to advancing the country as a whole.

The economy of Burkina Faso is primarily agricultural, with a significant portion of the population engaged in subsistence farming. Cotton is a major export, but the sector is vulnerable to fluctuations in global prices and climatic conditions. In recent years, there has been a push towards diversification, with mining (especially gold) becoming increasingly important. Yet, the benefits of this growth are not always evenly distributed, and rural areas, in particular, face significant development challenges.

And as I've mentioned throughout this book, the state of education in Burkina Faso reflects broader social and economic challenges. While there have been efforts to improve access to education, significant obstacles remain, particularly in rural areas. Limited infrastructure, insufficient educational materials, and a shortage of qualified teachers hinder the quality of education. Higher education and vocational training opportunities are also limited, impacting the workforce's ability to meet the demands of a modernizing economy.

At the core of our vision for Burkina Faso is a focus on leadership and entrepreneurship. We recognize that creating jobs and fostering economic growth requires more than just investment in businesses; it requires cultivating a generation of leaders and innovators who are prepared to drive change.

Our goal is to go to Africa and create jobs, but our vision extends further—to instill a culture of paying it forward. We are committed to nurturing entrepreneurs who, once successful, will invest in two more individuals, perpetuating a cycle of growth and support. This philosophy is not just about building businesses; it's about building communities of individuals who are equipped to create change.

I firmly believe that significant change does not require the efforts of all but rather the dedicated actions of a select few. I believe that it only takes 3% of people to achieve monumental shifts that will change the trajectory of Africa's future.

I am convinced that those individuals will come through Leading Change Africa – they will be the diamonds among us — rare, valuable, and capable of cutting through the toughest challenges to keep moving forward. They will create change if they're well trained, well equipped, and become well-rounded leaders.

To nurture these future leaders, we must focus on technology, innovation, and imparting practical knowledge in STEM (Science, Technology, Engineering, and Mathematics) fields. Creating jobs and advancing our economy will depend on our ability to equip our youth with the skills necessary to innovate and create. However, technical knowledge alone is insufficient to build a successful business. Understanding the intricacies of business is crucial to creating sustainable jobs and advancing Africa. Our accelerator program is designed to fill this gap, offering comprehensive training covering technical skills and business acumen, ensuring our graduates are prepared to thrive and lead.

It's a comprehensive program designed to guide budding entrepreneurs from idea generation to market implementation. We cover everything from technical skills in STEM fields to business management, ensuring our graduates are well-rounded and market-ready. This approach is about laying a foundation upon which sustainable businesses can be built, contributing to the broader economic fabric of Burkina Faso.

Upon graduating, we encourage our entrepreneurs to build their networks. While we remain a constant source of support, creating their own networks is crucial for their success. These networks serve as ecosystems of innovation, support, and opportunity, enabling our graduates to thrive and, in turn, support others.

Ousmane Nikiema, one of our Scholars, is a perfect example of a Leading Change Scholar creating change and paying it forward.

Ousmane is an extraordinary Scholar whose love for electronics began in the 8th grade. In Africa, Ousmane didn't have access to many of the electronics we have here in the United States. His fascination led to his determination to learn more and bring MORE access to his country.

However, despite his determination, the excessive university prices in his home country and his family's financial constraints presented a significant hurdle.

Everything changed when Ousmane was accepted and had the opportunity to work and study in the US through Leading Change Africa.

He shares, *"For me, getting the opportunity to work and study in the US was a blessing because it has helped me achieve my goals. Leading Change has helped me develop my English, mentored me to become a leader, motivated me to realize my entrepreneurial dream, and gave me computer typing skills. Before being accepted into the program, I didn't have access to computers, so I never learned how to type. Having this experience was really helpful."*

He went on to share that one of the most significant transformations he experienced was going from barely speaking English to having the courage and the ability to present in front of audiences of over

200 people!

He emphasized that he's not the only one with these dreams.

Access to higher education and personal development support provided by Leading Change Africa is a unique and invaluable opportunity for students like him in Africa.

He shared, *"I know it's not easy to support students like us in Africa, but we will always be grateful for Leading Change and the donors who support us. In addition to the financial support, the personal development we receive is really unique. The weekly meetings help me remember why I am here and why I should keep working hard to achieve my goals of developing Africa."*

The journey of our Scholars at Leading Change Africa, marked by their tenacity, drive, and commitment to community, serves not just as inspiration but as a call to action for each of us. Their stories underscore the profound impact that individual dedication to leadership, entrepreneurship, and social responsibility can have on our collective future. It's a vivid reminder that the path to significant change begins with personal commitment and action.

Their stories prompt a vital reflection: what steps are you taking to ensure that the next generation can thrive? How are you using your talents, knowledge, and resources to make a difference in your communities and beyond?

It's crucial to recognize that the story of change is one we all write together. Each decision you make, every challenge you overcome, and the ways in which you choose to lead and give back contribute to a larger picture. Our mission at Leading Change Africa is a testament to the power of collective action and visionary leadership. Still, it is your energy, innovation, and spirit that will drive us into the future.

Now, as we look to the future and opportunities for growth, I invite you to reflect on your role in this journey. How will you leverage your skills, passions, and dreams to pave the way for those who follow? The future of our communities, nations, and our world rests in the hands of empowered individuals like you, ready to lead, innovate, and impact.

What mark will you leave on the world?

"What legacy do you want to leave?"

10

Horizons of Hope: Building Africa's Next Generation of Innovators and Change Agents

Our emphasis on leadership and entrepreneurship reflects our belief that these are the pillars upon which the future of Burkina Faso will be built. We are not merely a scholarship program; we are a movement dedicated to empowering individuals with the skills, knowledge, and networks they need to succeed. By focusing on these areas, we aim to bring our country ahead of the curve in the next 10-20 years, driving sustainable change and prosperity.

The path to transforming Burkina Faso lies in addressing the multifaceted challenges of our current economic landscape with a forward-thinking approach to leadership and entrepreneurship.

Through our dedicated efforts to create jobs, empower the next generation, and foster a culture of innovation and self-reliance, we are laying the groundwork for a future where Burkina Faso stands as a beacon of progress and prosperity in Africa. This is our vision, commitment, and promise to the land that has given us so much.

Looking forward, Leading Change Africa is poised to embark on an ambitious expansion of our mission and impact. Our vision to transform 1,024 young Africans into leaders and change agents by 2030, with a ripple effect touching over 1 million lives by 2050, is both a goal and a promise. This vision is not merely about numbers; it's about deep, sustainable impact—cultivating a generation of leaders who are not only equipped to face the challenges of their time but are also committed to uplifting those around them.

To achieve this, we recognize the need to broaden our reach and deepen our impact. The stories of Scholars like Yankho Peaches remind us of the urgency of our mission. With hundreds of young Africans reaching out to us each year, hungering for the chance to change their destinies and their communities, expanding our capacity becomes not just an objective but a moral imperative.

Their stories are a testament to the power of support. For Scholars who've grown up in a world very different from ours, they only ever dream of the things we often take for granted.

It's hard to imagine life without clean, running water in your home, adequate electricity to charge your phone and your computer, or enough food to feed your family. From my time with Leading Change Africa, I've learned firsthand that these are the unimaginable barriers keeping bright young adults and their communities from reaching their potential.

Even when things are hard and feel out of reach, I've learned that the Leading Change Africa Scholars are filled with hope, courage, and the drive to keep going.

Yankho is a resilient young individual from Malawi. She is on our waiting list, hoping to be accepted into the Leading Change Africa program so she can attend school and pursue her dream of starting her own business.

Her story reflects the deep impact that education, mentorship, and opportunity can have on one's life.

Yankho shares that she's motivated to overcome all the doubts and challenges that have held her back so she can pursue a career in business management.

She discovered Leading Change as a platform that could provide the guidance, skills, and resources she needs for success!

Yankho said, *"The biggest challenge I have faced in my education is the financial challenges. Post-Secondary school and pursuing a career here in Africa is very expensive. Not only are the schools too expensive, but it's expensive to get the necessary equipment to attend and succeed in school."*

"If accepted into the Leading Change program, I see my life changing. I'll be able to get the guidance, skill sets, and resources to be competitive in the business world. It will not only change my life or help me, but it will be life-changing for other people. The kind of business I want to venture into will support my family and the community that I come from."

She envisions her journey with Leading Change as a force for positive change, not just in her life but in the lives of her family and the entire community.

The journey of Leading Change Africa offers invaluable insights for aspiring leaders and entrepreneurs. It underscores the importance of having a vision that extends beyond oneself—a vision that seeks to transform lives and communities. Our Scholars' stories exemplify what it means to embody resilience, to face seemingly insurmountable obstacles with determination, and to persist against all odds.

Let these stories be your guide and inspiration for those who dream of leading and innovating. Embrace the qualities of drive, determination, and resilience. Believe in your vision with unwavering conviction, and remember that true leadership is about creating paths for others to follow, learn, and grow.

As we set our sights on the future, we invite you to join us in this transformational journey. Whether you are a student, an aspiring entrepreneur, or a seasoned leader, there is a role for you in this change narrative. Your support, be it through mentorship, resources, or advocacy, can help fuel our expansion and empower more young Africans to achieve their dreams.

The future of Leading Change Africa is not just about scaling our programs but about inspiring a movement—a movement of individuals who are driven by a vision of a better world and determined to make it a reality. Together, we can forge a future where every young leader and entrepreneur has the opportunity to thrive, contribute, and make a lasting impact on the world.

What legacy do you want to leave? How will you use your drive, determination, and vision to inspire change? The future is in our hands, and together, we can shape it into one of prosperity, innovation, and leadership.

Acknowledgments

As I sit down to write these acknowledgments, I'm overwhelmed with gratitude and a profound sense of community. This book, a labor of love and a testament to the power of shared wisdom, would not have been possible without the incredible individuals who have traveled alongside me.

First, a heartfelt thank you to Faith Cheng, the incredible force behind the scenes, whose organizational skill and publishing expertise transformed the ideas into a seamless, refined masterpiece. Your relentless hard work and commitment to this project have truly been an inspiration.

To Kim Gillett and Ben Elikem, the creative geniuses on our marketing team, your vision, and talent have truly brought this book to life. From the unique cover design to the intricate marketing materials, your work has captured the essence of our shared journey in ways I could only dream of.

Hailey Krajewski, your ability to translate my experiences and insights into compelling stories has been invaluable. Your writing talent has given this book its heart and soul, and I am deeply thankful for your partnership in this endeavor.

John Leffin, Steve Wallman, and Professor Warfield, your mentorship has been a guiding light for me. Your wisdom, support, and encouragement have shaped my path and deeply enriched Leading Change Africa. I, nor the Scholars in our program, would be where we are today without your guidance and support.

David Gay, your insights and unwavering support have meant the world to me. Your influence is woven throughout these pages, and I am so grateful for your friendship and guidance.

And to all the incredible mentors who have graced my life and the pages of this book, your stories, and lessons have left an indelible mark on my journey. Your generosity in sharing your experiences has helped me grow and will inspire and guide readers for years to come.

This book celebrates the incredible power of mentorship, collaboration, and shared visions. From the bottom of my heart, thank you to everyone who has been a part of this journey. Your belief in this project and your contributions to its success have been the greatest gifts of all.

Made in the USA
Columbia, SC
27 June 2025